A Synodal Church

A Synodal Church

The Christian Faithful on Pilgrimage

Susan K. Wood

A Sheed & Ward Book

ROWMAN & LITTLEFIELD
Lanham • Boulder • New York • London

Rowman & Littlefield
Bloomsbury Publishing Inc, 1385 Broadway, New York, NY 10018, USA
Bloomsbury Publishing Plc, 50 Bedford Square, London, WC1B 3DP, UK
Bloomsbury Publishing Ireland, 29 Earlsfort Terrace, Dublin 2, D02 AY28, Ireland
www.rowman.com

Copyright © 2025 by The Rowman & Littlefield Publishing Group, Inc.

All rights reserved. No part of this publication may be: i) reproduced or transmitted in any form, electronic or mechanical, including photocopying, recording or by means of any information storage or retrieval system without prior permission in writing from the publishers; or ii) used or reproduced in any way for the training, development or operation of artificial intelligence (AI) technologies, including generative AI technologies. The rights holders expressly reserve this publication from the text and data mining exception as per Article 4(3) of the Digital Single Market Directive (EU) 2019/790.

An earlier version of Chapter One first appeared as "*Christifideles* within a Baptismal Ecclesiology: Reframing the Question of Participation in Leadership and Mission," *Studia Canonica* 58 (2024). Used with permission

British Library Cataloguing in Publication Information available

Library of Congress Cataloging-in-Publication Data Available

ISBN 9781538183168 (cloth : alk. paper) | ISBN 9781538183175 (pbk. : alk. paper) | ISBN 9781538183182 (ebook)

For product safety related questions contact productsafety@bloomsbury.com.

∞™ The paper used in this publication meets the minimum requirements of American National Standard for Information Sciences—Permanence of Paper for Printed Library Materials, ANSI/NISO Z39.48-1992.

Contents

Abbreviations		vii
Introduction		1
1	The Baptismal Foundations of a Synodal Church	7
2	A Synodal Church as a Pilgrim Church	27
3	Diversity within a Synodal Church	49
4	Spirituality for a Synodal, Pilgrim Church	71
5	A Culture of Dialogue	93
6	Beyond Dialogue: Discernment in Common	117
Index		141
About the Author		151

Abbreviations

AA	*Apostolicam Actuositatem*
AAS	*Acta Apostolicae Sedis*
AG	*Ad Gentes*
CIC	*Codex Iuris Canonici*
CL	*Christifideles Laici*
DH	*Dignitatis Humanae*
DV	*Dei Verbum*
EG	*Evangelii Gaudium*
EN	*Evangelii Nuntiandi*
ES	*Ecclesiam Suam*
GS	*Gaudium et Spes*
IL	*Instrumentum Laboris*
ITC	International Theological Commission
LG	*Lumen Gentium*
PG	*Patrologia Graeca*
PL	*Patrologia Latina*
PO	*Presbyterorum Ordinis*
SC	*Sacrosanctum Concilium*
SpEx	*Spiritual Exercises*
TI	*Theological Investigations*
UR	*Unitatis Redintegratio*

Introduction

The Synod on Synodality (2021–2024) launched the church into an experience of both *ressourcement*, a return to the sources of the church's tradition, and a*ggiornamento,* an updating or refreshing of the church's traditions, that had been the agenda of Vatican II. The synod, a specific event in the life of the church, became an initiation and education into a more purposeful way of being church according to a synodal modality. It represents an instance of *ressourcement* because this way of proceeding in the church is as old as the Council of Jerusalem (Acts 15:1–29) when that assembly determined what would be required of Gentile converts. It provides an example of *aggiornamento* because a synodal way of proceeding in the church responds to the enhanced appreciation of the dignity and missional responsibility of the baptized and to the experience of special synods convened since 1980, which highlight the array of regional variations the church encounters in its evangelical efforts.[1] The goal of a synodal way of proceeding in the church is to enable the church to better proclaim the Gospel to the diverse cultures and peoples it encounters. A synodal way of proceeding enables the church to accomplish its mission by ensuring the full, active, conscious participation of all the baptized in the mission of the church as they journey in communion with one another to their final union with God.

As Pope Francis has said, "Synodality is not a chapter in an ecclesiology textbook, much less a fad or a slogan to be bandied about in our meetings.

Synodality is an expression of the Church's nature, her form, style and mission."[2] A synodal church, much more than a document produced by a synod, is a style of being church that promotes "a way of being and working together, young and old, in listening and in discernment, in order to arrive at pastoral choices that respond to reality."[3] This book is a study in a synodal ecclesiology. Because this book goes to press between the first and second sessions of the Synod on Synodality (2021–2024), I make no pretensions of giving a complete account of this synod as an event in the life of the church, even though I incorporate material prepared for both sessions of the synod and the report from the first session. Nor is this a study of synodality as such. We often hear of a synodal church as being a pilgrim church, as being diverse, as incorporating dialogue and discernment. These descriptors are not new. My contribution is to probe the theological foundations of these characteristics of a synodal pilgrim church, the spirituality that sustains it, and the practices of dialogue and discernment inherent to this way of being church and to show how they intersect and are operative in this modality of being church.

One hears everywhere today that a synodal church is grounded in baptism. Those of us involved in the ecumenical movement have long recognized this sacrament's importance for the mutual recognition of one another's inherent dignity and equality and its importance for our communion in Christ. This book goes beyond my 2009 study, *One Baptism: Ecumenical Dimensions of the Doctrine of Baptism*,[4] to basically say that there is no such thing as laity in the church, but only Christians, some of whom are ordained, and all of whom have their own particular ordo or place in the church as a community of missionary disciples. A synodal ecclesiology begins with the equality of all the people of God and a consideration of the church before into any division of states of life or ministry. From this perspective, synodality and conciliarity are attributes of the church before they are exercises of any particular ministry. Within a baptismal ecclesiology the church is an ordered communion of a diversity of ministries, and hierarchy is seen to be a liturgical concept with ministry serving the people of God. Rather than a strict division between the sacred, associated with ordained ministry, and secularity, associated with the laity, the entire church within a baptismal ecclesiology has a secular mission—the transformation of the world into the reign of God.

My focus on a baptismal ecclesiology here does not intend to downplay the importance of the Eucharist in the church, for baptism leads directly to the Eucharistic table and deputes the Christian people to Eucharistic worship. All ministry, however, including that of the ordained priesthood, is first baptismal before ensuing specifications received through other sacraments, states of life, or instituted ministries. This is because both baptism and the Eucharist are sacramental celebrations of the one paschal mystery of Christ, his dying and rising, under two sacramental modalities, one employing the real symbolism of womb and tomb, rebirth and dying and rising with Christ, and the other the real symbolism of his body broken and blood poured out for us and our salvation. A baptismal and a Eucharistic ecclesiology should never be in competition with one another, but perhaps it is time for more emphasis on baptism and for questioning from a baptismal perspective the binary lay-ordained that has dominated our theological imaginations for so long in favor of an ecclesiology of the people of God as an ordered communion.

The chapter on a synodal church as a pilgrim church necessarily follows upon the chapter that identifies the church as the people of God forged in baptism. The category "people of God" situates the church in history within a journey to a final destination of union with God, but also to a destination in terms of the mission it is to accomplish on the way. A pilgrim journey entails growth and development, and purification and transformation. As true as this is for individuals, it equally applies to a pilgrim church. History shows us that this process of reform, growth, and transformation is not new, but has always characterized the church, which is *simul sancta et semper purificanda*, at once holy and yet always needing to be purified (*LG* 8).[5] The necessity and fact of reform point to the need for discernment, a vital characteristic of a synodal church, to distinguish between true and false reform in the church.

The need for a chapter on diversity became evident once the pilgrim people are seen as firmly planted within history. This is not diversity out of political correctness or diversity for diversity's sake, but simply the nature of a church embedded in history working to evangelize the people in those times and places and to transform those contexts into the reign of God. Because diversity has theological and not merely sociological import, it needs to correlate with a theological description of the church as a communion.

"Communion ecclesiology" has rightly been criticized as being a polyvalent term meaning different things to different people. The diversity of a synodal church requires the identification of a communion ecclesiology that does not subsume this diversity into an overarching unity that actually erases diversity in the end, because it assumes diversity into a monolithic unity that is then imposed globally. Nevertheless, I consider communion to be a helpful conceptualization of the church if one is clear about what one means by it. I use two concepts derived from economic theories of the exchange of goods to offer a conceptual framework for envisioning diversity within a synodal church: "globalization" and "*mondialisation.*" I argue that the concept of globalization correlates with John Paul II's concept of ecclesial communion, while *mondialisation* represents a different model of communion more in line with Francis's thinking.[6]

Diversity requires ecclesial structures adaptable to local contexts that also maintain communion within the diversity. Recent modifications of the Synod of Bishops and renewed attention to episcopal conferences enhance church structures to facilitate the ecclesial communion of diverse regional variations within the church. The possibility of diversity in ministries is actualized in recent modifications of instituted lay ministries and potentially possible for ordained ministry once true discernment processes are implemented by regional synods or episcopal conferences.

Spirituality is the "soul" of a synodal church. The journey of the pilgrim in communion with others is a journey of conversion and transformation sustained and nourished by life in the Spirit and a baptismal and Eucharistic spirituality and enacted in virtues. The spiritual growth is one of increasing personal and communal freedom from internal and external obstacles that get in the way of proclaiming the Gospel and of accomplishing the ministry of reconciliation entrusted to everyone in the church (2 Cor 5:18–20). While a spirituality generally describes individuals, a synodal church embodies a communal ecclesial spirituality that mirrors that of individuals, appropriate for a church that is first the people of God before it is institutional. Virtues of mercy and ecclesial humility enable a synodal, pilgrim church to accompany the sinner, the marginalized, the weak, and those who suffer even as it itself follows a path of conversion.

While the first four chapters focus on the nature of a synodal church, in the last two chapters I turn to two specific practices inherent to synodality—dialogue and discernment. Dialogue has been a particular focus in the church both since Paul VI's *Ecclesiam Suam* and also since the church's involvement in the ecumenical movement right after the Second Vatican Council. Dialogue occurs within several registers—dialogue with God, within the church, and with the world, culture, and other faith traditions. Within the church, dialogue makes possible an ecclesiology of communion and is the hallmark of a synodal church.

From my long experience in ecumenical dialogues with Lutherans, the Orthodox, and Baptists, I think synodality casts dialogue in a slightly different light in terms of different processes of spiritual conversations incorporating active listening and intentional speaking. By fostering a culture of dialogue, a synodal church stands as a prophetic witness in a society that has become increasingly uncivil. For a synodal church, dialogue, more than a way of proceeding within the church, is the primary way of carrying out the apostolic mission of the church in the contemporary world. Dialogue becomes more essential in a pluralistic culture as well as in a diverse church to create communion, at least in understanding, across differences.

Finally, once I finished the chapter on dialogue, I realized that discernment in common is the step beyond dialogue that enables a synodal church to be aware of the movements of the Spirit and thereby find the will of God in the concrete circumstances of a particular time and place. Building on an analysis of contemporary reality and a reading of the "signs of the times," discernment enables the church to sift through what needs to be purified in its life, what needs reform, and what is needed to come to a communal decision for concrete action. The theological foundations of the practice of discernment lie in a theology of charisms, those gifts of the Spirit for the upbuilding of the church, in a theology of the *sensus fidei* (sense of the faith) and the *sensus fidelium* (sense of the faithful) that epistemologically represent a kind of knowledge operative through connaturality. This book concludes by outlining some processes of discernment in common as well as the necessary prerequisites to engage in this practice. When practiced at multiple levels of ecclesial life, discernment in common has the potential of being a transformative ecclesial practice, enabling the church to be more effective in its mission.

In developing the baptismal basis for a synodal church, the nature of this church as a pilgrim embedded in history and on a journey of growth and transformation, a church characterized by diversity, sustained spiritually, and engaging in practices of dialogue and discernment, this book aims to provide the theological foundations for a synodal church and to flesh out those characteristics of a synodal church that became so evident through the work of the Synod on Synodality.

ACKNOWLEDGMENTS

I would like to thank Eugene Schlesinger, who was kind enough to read drafts of all the chapters and offer helpful feedback; and John McLaughlin, who checked this systematic theologian's use of Hebrew terms. My gratitude also goes to Richard Brown from Rowman & Littlefield, who invited me to undertake this project and who encouraged me to "follow my instincts," and to his editorial staff who guided the manuscript to completion. The students, faculty, and administration at the Regis St. Michael's Faculty of Theology in the Toronto School of Theology at the University of Toronto also receive my gratitude for helping me to make—and hopefully live—the connections between theology and ministry, mission and scholarship. Finally, I would not be doing any of this unless my religious community, the Sisters of Charity of Leavenworth, Kansas, had not had the vision, faith, and trust to permit me to follow my vocation to be a theologian.

NOTES

1. The concluding document or the apostolic exhortation following the eleven special synods focusing on problems relating directly to specific churches or regions from 1980 to 2019 are: "Conclusions of the Special Synod of the Bishops of the Netherlands" (1980), First Special Assembly for Europe, "We Are Witnesses of Christ Who Has Delivered Us" (1991), *Ecclesia in Africa* (1995), *Ecclesia in Libanon* (1997), *Ecclesia in America* (1999), *Ecclesia in Asia* (1999), *Ecclesia in Oceania* (1999), *Ecclesia in Europa* (2003), *Africae munus* (2011), *Ecclesia in Medio Oriente* (2012), *Querida Amazonia* (2020).

2. Francis, "We Are Church Together," Address to the Faithful of the Diocese of Rome, September 18, 2021, in Dicastery for Communication, *Walking Together: The Way of Synodality* (Maryknoll, NY: Orbis, 2023), 151–63, at 152.

3. Francis, "A Way of Being and Working Together," Angelus, Saint Peter's Square, October 28, 2018, in Dicastery for Communication, *Walking Together: The Way of Synodality*, 77.

4. Susan K. Wood, *One Baptism: Ecumenical Dimensions of the Doctrine of Baptism* (Collegeville, MN: Liturgical Press, 2009).

5. Second Vatican Council, Dogmatic Constitution on the Church, *Lumen Gentium*, November 21, 1964, https://www.vatican.va/archive/hist_councils/ii_vatican_council/documents/vat-ii_const_19641121_lumen-gentium_en.html. Hereafter *LG*.

6. *Mondialisation*, often translated in English as globalization because no equivalent exists in English, differs from globalization. *Mondialisation* (literally worldwide-ization) refers to an interdependence and cooperation among countries that retain their cultural identities and exchange their cultural artifacts, services, information, and goods within an international network of different countries. The United Nations would be an example of *mondialisation*. Globalization, generally considered to be a stage beyond *mondialisation*, is a movement that tends toward the dissolution of national identities and the abolishment of borders inside the world network of free economic exchanges associated with capitalism. Globalization tends to homogenization, while *mondialisation* retains cultural differences and identities.

1

The Baptismal Foundations of a Synodal Church

Baptism provides the sacramental basis for a synodal church because baptism establishes the new people of God, reborn from water and the Holy Spirit. As Walter Kasper observes, "people of God" expresses the pilgrim nature of "the being-on-the-way in history of God's people and, at the same time, God's being with us and among us on this way."[1] Synodality is a way-of-being church that adds specificity to the concept of a pilgrim church because a church on pilgrimage is traveling together, reflecting the etymology of the word "synod" referring to a shared path or journey together.[2] In this sense we can speak of a synodal church and identify its contours and activities, which are ongoing in the life of the church apart from an event called a synod. Finally, this pilgrim church situated in history travels on a journey toward its destiny, the kingdom of God and final eschatological fulfillment (*LG* 9). This dynamic description of the church will have implications for the development and change inherent to a pilgrim church.

Baptism establishes the fundamental equality and unity of the people of God prior to divisions into various ministries and states of life and prior to a division between ordained ministers and lay people, reflecting the structure of *Lumen Gentium*, in which chapter 2 on the people of God precedes the following chapter on the hierarchical church and subsequent chapters on the laity and religious life. A baptismally based ecclesiology gives us an ecclesiology that begins with what is shared in common rather than with what is distinctive, and with baptism rather than the Eucharist as the paradigm for ecclesial identity. The result is a theology of the *Christifideles,* the Christian faithful, preceding a theology of the laity or a theology of ordination. Reflection beginning with the *Christifideles* bypasses the binary pair "hierarchy-laity," replacing it with the binary "community-charisms/ministers."[3] As Bruno Forte comments, the first binary emphasizes the distinction between the laity and the clergy even though they are fundamentally united by baptism, while the second binary highlights the unity of the baptized without denying the variety represented by the gifts of the Spirit.[4] A baptismal ecclesiology provides the framework for such a shift in perspective. Synodality reflects this unity as an attribute of the people of God as a whole before synods are events in the life of the church or a governing structure of the church.

Any discussion of the church, especially an ecclesiology for a synodal church, must begin with its mission, for the mission of the church identifies the purpose and destination of the pilgrim church. The church does not have a mission; it is a mission in its very identity.[5] This mission can broadly be described as the transformation of the world into the reign of God as inaugurated in the person of Jesus Christ, who came to extend God's saving mercy and proclaim the advent of the kingdom of God (Mk 1:9–15; Lk 3:21–4:14). Jesus's message was the transformation foretold in Isaiah 61:1–2: good news brought to the poor, captives released, the blind given sight, and the oppressed freed. The entire church participates in that mission, for each one of the people of God is an active subject in the church and, as a missionary disciple, is responsible for the church's mission. A synodal church confirms the agency of each person and promotes their full, active, and conscious participation in the church.

THE *CHRISTIFIDELES* WITHIN A BAPTISMAL ECCLESIOLOGY

The term "people of God," which originates in the Old Testament with reference to the Israelites (see Ex 6:7; Lv 26:12; Jer 32:38; Ezr 11:20; Ps 135), is applied to the church in the New Testament (see Acts 15:14, 18:10; Rom 9:25f; 2 Cor 6:16). One enters this new people of God through baptism. The inclusivity of this people fulfills the promise made to Abraham which is universal in scope to include all nations (see Gn 18:18; 22:18; 26:4; 28:14). Described by its relationship to the Trinity, the new people of God is established by the new covenant ratified in Christ and has Christ as its head, possesses the dignity and freedom of the daughters and sons of God, and is where the Holy Spirit dwells in the hearts of this people as in a temple (*LG* 9). It is a people on the move, for "its destiny is the kingdom of God" (*LG* 9). The people of God are not just any people, but the people that God has elected, God's chosen people (1 Pt 2:9–10). This people, called together by God, is known by the God who elects them, the God whom this people serves and worships.

Lumen Gentium describes this people as a communion, a seed and sacrament of saving unity (*LG* 9). Even though scattered throughout the world and present in all the nations of the earth, the members of this people are in communion with each other (*LG* 13). Within this communion all spiritual and temporal resources are shared (*LG* 13). Even salvation occurs communally, for God "has, however, willed to women and men holy and to save them, not as individuals without any bond between them, but rather to make them into a people who might acknowledge him and serve him in holiness" (*LG* 9; *AG* 2). This communion includes not only the wayfarers on earth, but also those who "sleep in the peace of Christ" (*LG* 49). The union of these two groups is reinforced by "an exchange of spiritual goods" in such a way that we can speak of a thin veil separating the living from the dead within the communion of saints, and the mutual aid and assistance exchanged between them.

That Christians become members of this new people of God and priests through baptism is reflected in the liturgy of baptism. The General Introduction to the Catholic rite of baptism refers to 1 Peter 2:9, where it states that "baptism is the sacrament by which its recipients are incorporated into the Church and are built up together in the Spirit into a house where God lives, into a holy nation and a royal priesthood."[6] The prayer that accompanies the anointing with chrism associates the baptized with the threefold office of Christ: "He now anoints you with the chrism of salvation so that, united with his people, you may remain for ever a member of Christ who is Priest, Prophet, and King."[7]

This theme of the threefold office of Christ applied to all the faithful dates from the early church. Eusebius, the fourth-century bishop of Caesarea and chronicler of the early church, comments that among the Jews, high priests, kings, and prophets were anointed, thus making them *christs*.[8] While the evidence for anointing prophets is rather thin, the only Old Testament references being Psalm 105:15, cited in 1 Chronicles 16:22 and 1 Kings 19:16, Jesus Christ is clearly and directly identified as High Priest (Heb 3:1) and King (Jn 18:33–37, 19:14–22). Disciples, although none of the Twelve, identify Jesus as a prophet in John 4:19, 6:14, and 9:17. In Acts 3:22–26 the implication is that Jesus is a prophet like Moses. Jesus seems to refer to himself as a prophet in Luke 4:24 by the words, "No prophet is accepted in his native place."

The theme of the royal priesthood figures in the writing of a number of Church Fathers. St. Irenaeus asserted that "all the just possess a priestly rank."[9] Chrysostom applies the role of priest, prophet, and king to all the faithful in his commentary on 2 Corinthians 1:21–22.[10] This passage from Paul, however, does not make this application, but only speaks of an anointing. St. Augustine's commentary on Luke 5:33 says, "We are all priests according to justice, we who are consecrated by the oil of joy for the kingdom and for the priesthood."[11] The early fifth-century bishop, Fastidius, applies the threefold pattern to the Christian faithful on the basis of their having been anointed in baptism like Christ the anointed one.[12]

One study of the triad "priest, prophet, and king" concludes that "none of the texts cited from the first twelve hundred years of the Church's history applies the three as titles or as characteristics of the ministry of the ordained."[13] The earliest use of the threefold title "priest, prophet, and king" applied first to Christ, then to the church as a whole for the first twelve hundred years of the church's history before later referring to ordained ministers. This means that it applies to the people of God before it designates the office of the ordained, another sign of the priority accorded the people of God as a whole.

Further attributes of the people of God are given in 1 Peter 2:9–10, which applies the prerogatives of ancient Israel among the nations to the Christian people: "But you are a chosen race, a royal priesthood, a holy nation, God's own people, in order that you may proclaim the mighty acts of him who called you out of darkness into his marvellous light." These words immediately point to the value and dignity of each member of the church who has "been born anew, not of perishable but of imperishable seed through the living and enduring word of God" (1 Pt 1:23). This new people is born not of flesh, but from water and the Holy Spirit (Jn 3:5–6). This messianic people has as its head Christ, who is the high priest (Heb 5:5) and makes the new people "a kingdom of priests" (Rv 1:6) to serve and worship the Father. All those who constitute the people of God and are embodied in Christ in baptism are thereby also made "temples of the Holy Spirit" (1 Cor 6:19) or "temples of God" (1 Cor 3:16, 17; 2 Cor 6:16) and members of Christ (Rom 12:5; 1 Cor 12:13, 27).

From these early texts, we can see that the term *Christifideles* includes a number of concepts: a people consecrated to God and set apart by God's election; the unitary nature of the community founded on a common baptism; participation in the triple office of Christ as priest, prophet, and king; and the universal call to holiness. The identity of this community is shared by all subsequent grouping within it, whether those groups be identified as the laity, the clergy, monks, or apostolic religious. Later differentiation of identities within the community do not abrogate this primary identity. For example, the sacramental character received in ordination does not replace or negate the sacramental character received in baptism.

ORDERING THE BAPTISMAL COMMUNITY

Baptism orders the church as does the Sacrament of Holy Orders. Orthodox theologians Nicholas Afanasiev and John Zizioulas speak of baptism and chrismation as an ordination, through the laying on of hands with prayer to the Holy Spirit, into the royal priesthood.[14] This ordination, not to be confused with the sacrament of Orders, enables the baptized and chrismated Christians to participate in the Eucharistic assembly and also enables one to differentiate various positions and relationships within this liturgical assembly.[15] As Zizioulas expresses it, "the baptized person does not simply become a 'Christian,' as we tend to think, but he becomes *a member of a particular 'ordo'* in the eucharistic community."[16] In his view, this application of ordination to the baptized is essential to a theology of the laity, for "once this is forgotten, it is easy to speak of the laity as 'non-ordained' and thus arrive at the possibility . . . of either making the layman an unnecessary element in the Eucharistic community (hence the 'private mass' and the entire issue of clericalism) or of making him the basis of all 'orders,' as if he himself were not a defined order but a generic source or principle."[17] This baptismal ordination is constitutive of the church, the community that is the "existential 'locus' of the convergence of the charismata" (1 Cor 12).[18]

Afanasiev contributes to this concept of a baptismal ordination by distinguishing "lay people," those who are not consecrated and are not the people of God, from "laics," who are the members of God's people. Thus, he prefers to speak of a "laic" rather than a "layperson." Baptismal ordination is not an ordination of lay people, but of "laics," that is, the members of God's people.[19] Afanasiev interprets this ordination saying, "The newly baptized, spiritually born in the sacrament of baptism, is ordained for service in the Church, for carrying out his calling as a member of God's people, a nation of kings and priests."[20] Thus the church consists of those who are ordained, and a lay person cannot be viewed in opposition to the consecrated but only in opposition to the non-consecrated, that is, to those who are not in the church or members of God's people.[21] Theologically, Afanasiev says, "there can be no 'lay people' in the church."[22] By this he means that there is no non-consecrated person in the church. He understands lay people as the "non-consecrated" as contrasted with the "consecrated," which includes all those who belong to the priesthood. He does not mean that there is no distinction between the ordained and the non-ordained. Thus, the term "lay ordination" is itself a contradiction because the non-consecrated do not have an ordo within the consecrated people.[23]

The Eucharistic assembly, the paradigm for the notion of "order" in the church, requires the special ministry of a presider. Afanasiev identifies the charism of presidency as distinguishing presiders from the rest of the church in the early church.[24] He affirms the ontological necessity of a bishop as presider, but staunchly resists the notion that this role stands in opposition to the royal priesthood, a priesthood which the bishop shares.

In his opinion, the scholastic theologians distanced themselves from the common priesthood through an unfounded fear of undermining the hierarchical character of the church. Furthermore, when some Protestants moved away from the ministry of the bishop and affirmed the universal priesthood, Catholics emphasized the ministerial priesthood, and the discussion of the common priesthood remained comparatively undeveloped until the mid-twentieth century. Afanasiev holds the two together in a necessary relationship, the ministerial priesthood being impossible apart from the royal priesthood of all the baptized, and the royal priesthood requiring an ordering of the charisms within it.

The concept of baptism as a kind of ordination contributes to a theology of the church as an "ordered communion" in which baptism and ministerial ordination establish an ecclesial "re-positioning" of persons within the Eucharistic assembly and thus the church.[25] Within this construct, the church is an "ordered communion," a network of relationships within a ministerial community carrying on the mission entrusted by Christ. Within this baptismal community, all public ministries carry out service to God's people according to their particular ordo within the community. All are equal in dignity within a diversity of ministerial roles and ecclesial repositioning.

THE PEOPLE OF GOD IN THE EUCHARISTIC ASSEMBLY

A baptismal ecclesiology beginning with a theology of the *Christifideles* provides a theology of the people of God distinguished by various charisms and ministries. Such an ecclesiology, far from excluding the Eucharist, actually leads to it starting from the identity and mission of the entire people of God. This becomes more evident when baptisms are celebrated during the Eucharistic liturgy with the parish assembled. The first mission of the consecrated people of God is to give worship to God. This occurs first and foremost in the liturgy of the Eucharist. The ordination of baptism gives the baptized their place in the Eucharistic assembly and deputes them to participate in the official worship of the church. Thus, baptism and the Eucharist are intimately related, the first oriented to the second. The completion that the Eucharist brings to baptism is twofold: first, the visible, ongoing sacramental communion in the body of Christ, the same body in which we already participate in baptism, and second, the visible communion both with a local church and, through the local church, with the other Eucharistic communions.

The priestly people can properly be considered to be concelebrants of the Eucharist since the whole assembly inclusive of the presider and the people are the subjects of the liturgical action.[26] Only the ordained minister, however, is the presider. Catholic documents provide ample evidence for the whole community being the subject of the liturgical action. The *General Instruction of the Roman Missal* regards the entire assembly as the primary agent of the liturgical action, for the celebration of the Eucharist is the action of Christ and the Church (§19).[27] The *Catechism of the Catholic Church* also emphasizes that, "it is the whole *community*, the Body of Christ united with its Head, that celebrates" (§1140). *Lumen Gentium* states that the priestly community "offer[s] to God the divine victim and themselves along with him; and so both in this offering and in holy communion all fulfill their own part in the liturgical action" (*LG* 11). This community also exercises its priesthood "in receiving the sacraments, in prayer and thanksgiving, through the witness of a holy life, by self-denial and by active charity" (*LG* 10).

The liturgical assembly is an ordered community reflecting an ordered church. Thus, there should be a reciprocal relationship between relationships within the liturgy and within the church as a whole. "Full, active participation" in the liturgy translates into a participative church wherein all the members have a voice. This is not a democratic, but a liturgical principle. Such participation does not negate role differentiation in the church any more than it does within the liturgy, but it signals the desirability of a more inclusive role for non-ordained members in councils and synods.

From another perspective, the International Theological Commission in its text, "*Sensus Fidei* in the Life of the Church," also argues that the faithful "are not merely passive recipients of what the hierarchy teaches and theologians explain; rather they are living and active subjects within the Church."[28] Historically, they played "an active role in the development of Christian belief," that is, in the development of doctrine, "even when theologians and bishops were divided on the issue."[29] Moreover, "sometimes, when the Church came to a definition, the *Ecclesia docens* had clearly 'consulted' the faithful, and it pointed to the *consensus fidelium* as one of the arguments which legitimated the definition."[30] Consequently, the ITC document suggests that the old distinction between the teaching church (*ecclesia docens*) and the learning church (*ecclesia dicens*) is no longer theologically appropriate.[31] All the faithful are both teachers and learners, although the magisterium has a distinct responsibility to discern, discriminate, define, promulgate, and enforce teaching as it applies to the entire church.[32] They judge "whether opinions present among the people of God, and which may seem to be the *sensus fidelium*, actually corresponds to the truth of the Tradition received from the Apostles."[33] All discern and the magisterium, in addition to discerning, judges.

UNITY AND DIFFERENTIATION WITHIN THE PEOPLE OF GOD

The unity within the people of God is found in several characteristics of this people. The terms *"Christifideles"* and "the people of God" unequivocally apply to all the baptized before there is further distinction within the community. Both terms pick up the notion of a people consecrated to God and set apart by God's election. The unitary nature of the community is founded on a common baptism and confirmation, on participation in the triple office of Christ as priest, prophet, and king, and on the universal call of all the faithful to holiness.

Nevertheless, there is also differentiation within the people of God, and several distortions in the relationship between the one and the many, between unity and differentiation are possible. There can be, for instance: a clericalism whereby those who are ordained are regarded as superior to other members; a democratization that does not sufficiently appreciate the ordained ministry itself; or a professionalization which regards as the responsibility of certain individuals tasks in which all should participate.

Differentiation also arises from the charisms of the *Christifideles* (1 Cor 12:7; 14:26) and by the various ministries exercised by this people, both serving to build up the community. The charisms of the *Christifideles* are associated with their share in the prophetic role of Christ. The charisms enable them to be living witnesses through lives of faith and charity. The manifestation of the Spirit received by each person is given for the common good (1 Cor 12:7; *LG* 12). The charisms "equip the saints for the work of ministry, for building up the body of Christ, until all of us come to the unity of the faith and of the knowledge of the Son of God, to maturity, to the measure of the full stature of Christ" (Eph 4:11–12).

Ministries within the people of God also vary. Ministries serving the community include apostles, prophets, and teachers, who exercise deeds of power, gifts of healing, forms of assistance, forms of leadership, and the ability to speak and to understand various kinds of tongues (1 Cor 12:27). Various ministries mentioned in the New Testament include the roles of ministers (1 Cor 4:1; 2 Cor 3:6; 6:4), presidents (Rom 12:8; 1 Thes 5:12; Heb 13:7, 17, 24; Acts 12:1; 20:28), pastors (Eph 4:11), elders (Ti 1:5), and teachers (Acts 12:1; 1 Cor 12:18). Through the gifts of the Spirit and various ministries, the building up of the church is the common work of all the members of the body, who are equal in dignity and value.[34]

In the contemporary church, both ordained and lay ministries contribute to the ordering of the people of God. Ordained ministry in the church, while embodying a charism of the Holy Spirit, is also a sacrament of the church that orders the community insofar as it repositions an individual within the community to perform activities in the person and name of Christ and the church.[35] The instituted ministries of acolyte, lector, and catechist are official lay ministries arising from baptism and confirmation that also order the community through public, officially instituted ministry.[36] The "orders" of religious communities and various states of life represent yet another kind of ordering of the people of God.

SECULARITY OF THE *CHRISTIFIDELES* IN AN ECCLESIAL CONTEXT

Conciliar and post-conciliar Roman Catholic documents identify the ecclesial condition of the laity as inseparable from their baptismal state and to their secular nature. A theology of the *Christifideles*, however, will extend this secular mission to all the baptized. Referring to the subgroup "laity" within the *Christifideles*, *Lumen Gentium* states, "The laity have their own special character which is secular" (*LG* 31). *Apostolicam Actuositatem*, the Decree on the Apostolate of the Laity, reiterates this point saying, "Laypeople should take the restoration of the temporal order as their proper function" (*AA* 7). The *Lineamenta* for the Synod of Bishops entitled "Vocation and Mission of the Laity in the Church and in the World Twenty Years after the Second Vatican Council" likewise states that "the same Council presents the participation of the laity in temporal and worldly affairs, that is their 'secularity,' not only as a sociological datum, but also and specifically as a theological and ecclesial datum, as the characteristic form of living the Christian vocation."[37]

John Paul II's Apostolic Exhortation, *Christifideles Laici* (*CL*), however, develops the notion of secularity in terms of the whole church while maintaining the distinctive contributions of various groups in the church to this when it says, "Certainly all the members of the Church are sharers in this secular dimension but in different ways" (*CL* 15).[38] This arguably represents a development beyond *Lumen Gentium* and more in line with *Gaudium et Spes*. Nevertheless, *Christifideles Laici* continues to reiterate the identification of the laity with the secular: "In particular the sharing of the lay faithful has its own manner of realization and function, which, according to the Council, is 'properly and particularly' theirs. Such manner is designated with the expression 'secular character'" (*CL* 15).

While the secular responsibilities of the laity are indisputable insofar as many instances exist where only they can provide witness in the workplace, in families, and within the professional, social, political, and cultural life of society, focus on the laity with at times an almost exclusive emphasis on their secularity rather than on the *Christifideles* has had several unfortunate effects. First, it has tended to bifurcate the world and the church, the profane and the sacred, and the laity and the ordained. Second, it has obscured the fact that the whole church has a secular mission.

Third, at least in the early days of the phenomenon, it made the concept of lay ministry in the church seem extraordinary at the same time it occasioned multiple cautious warnings lest the priesthood of the baptized usurp or be confused with the ministerial priesthood. Even today, the relationship between lay ecclesial ministers and ordained clergy can be strained as both groups navigate their respective ministerial roles and identities.

The church as a whole has a secular mission, not just the group identified as "laity" within it. The people of God are "sent as a mission to the world as the light of the world and the salt of the earth (see Mt 5:13–16)" (*LG* 9). *Gaudium et Spes*, for example, describes the interpenetration of the church and the world, stating that "the church . . . proceeds on its way with the whole of humanity and shares the world's earthy lot, while also being a leaven and a sort of soul of human society, which is to be renewed in Christ and transformed into God's family" (*GS* 40).[39]

Paul VI recognized this secular mission of the church, saying that the church "has an authentic secular dimension inherent to her inner nature and mission, which is deeply rooted in the mystery of the Word Incarnate, and which is realized in different forms through her members."[40] Henri de Lubac uses a similar reference to the Incarnation to describe the relationship between nature and grace: "for the two elements which we deal with here, nature and the supernatural, have not become an intermixture or confusion but have been joined in intimate union in dependence on and in the image of the two natures in Christ."[41] Relating the secular mission of the church to the incarnation of the Word in history describes the church/world and nature/grace relationship more in terms of a *circuminsessio* or a *perichoresis* than a two-story hierarchical universe.[42] The world is transformed as nature is transformed.[43] The image may also be apt to describe the relationship of the various charisms, ministries, and states of life within the *Christifideles*. Such an image removes the hierarchical image of "elevation" and any notion that one ministry or state in life is superior to another. Within the diversity whose source is the Spirit of unity, all work together to build up the body of Christ.

The church's mission and thus the mission of the *Christifideles* is ultimately the transformation of the world into the reign of God. Jesus proclaimed the advent of the kingdom of God (Mk 1:9–15; Lk 3:21–4:14) identifying the transformation foretold by Isaiah 61:1–2: good news brought to the poor, captives released, the blind given sight, and the oppressed freed. The kingdom was present in the person of Jesus (Lk 4:21). The mission of the church continues this mission of Jesus inaugurated at his baptism and assumed by Christians in their own baptisms in which they put on Christ and participate in his death and resurrection. The mission of the church, related to the royal priesthood, is prior to the missions of individual members of the church. As *Presbyterorum Ordinis*, the Decree on the Ministry and Life of Priests, affirms, within the mystical body all the faithful share in the anointing of the Spirit, are formed into a holy and royal priesthood, offer spiritual sacrifices to God through Christ, and have a part to play in the mission of the whole body.[44]

This mission is also expressed in *Lumen Gentium*'s description of the church as a sort of sacrament, that is, a sign and instrument "of intimate union with God and of the unity of all humanity" (*LG* 1).[45] The church is a sign for nations, thus it is a mission *ad extra* and encompasses both the historical reality of human community now and union with God now, but it is also oriented eschatologically to ultimate union and the definitive union of humanity when recapitulated in Christ at the end time. The church in its most basic identity is not simply a faith movement, but rather what might be called a sacramental reality, in which God works actively in and through human beings and actions in the midst of a concrete, historical community.

Any description of the secularity of the laity does not preclude their ministry within the church. Conversely, the ordained priesthood, not losing what it receives through baptism and confirmation, is also called to minister in the world, albeit in forms compatible with its ministerial identity. Thus, there can be no strict dualism between secularity and the sacred, a secular Christian and a spiritual person, or world and church. The transformation of the world is the vocation of the whole church, and all Christians are active subjects in the church working for that transformation.

IMPLICATIONS FOR CONCILIARITY AND SYNODALITY

The identity of the whole church as participating in the threefold office of Christ as a priestly, prophetic, and kingly Messianic community in baptism as well as the inerrancy of the people of God as a whole in matters of faith bear implications for conciliarity and synodality.[46] Just as the trilogy of priest, prophet, and king is attributed to the entire community before it is used to characterize individual offices or states of life within that community, so too, synodality and conciliarity are attributes of the church as a whole before they are seen as exercises of any particular ministry.

While the term "conciliarity" primarily refers to a gathering of bishops exercising their pastoral office, the Orthodox–Catholic ecumenical document known as the Ravenna statement affirms the possibility of "taking the term in a more comprehensive sense to refer to all the members of the Church (cf. the Russian term *sobornost*)" and "as signifying that each member of the Body of Christ, by virtue of baptism, has his or her place and proper responsibility in eucharistic koinonia."[47] While the Eucharist has rightfully been identified as manifesting this order and koinonia within the ecclesial community, a baptismal ecclesiology of the people of God endowed with various charisms likewise provides a theological foundation for conciliarity.

Conciliarity is manifested in the local church gathered around its bishop, in regional groupings of neighboring local churches, and in the entire or whole church (*Ecclesia universa*).[48] In each case, there is no church except in Christian believers and their assemblies, for the church is the *congregatio* (*convocatio*) *fidelium*, those identified as God's own people in 1 Peter 2:9–10.[49] These people, regardless of their office or state in life, are together *synodoi*, "travel companions."[50] Synodality and conciliarity are aspects of the entire church before they are activities of the church's hierarchy. Theologically grounded in the identity of the people and modelled on the Trinitarian communion, a koinonia without any diminution or subordination,[51] synodality and conciliarity imply the participation of all the people of God.

The Ravenna statement identifies conciliarity primarily with the local church, described as "synodal" or "conciliar" in structure (§20), but states that the composition of a formally designated regional synod is always essentially episcopal, even when it includes other members of the church, with only bishops having a deliberative voice (§25). Despite the episcopal character of regional synods, their conciliarity or synodality involves the entire churches of the assembled bishops in two respects. First, the bishops "are bearers of and give voice to the faith" of the churches (§38). Second, the decisions of a council must be recognized through a reception "according to which the people of God as a whole—by means of reflection, discernment, discussion and prayer—acknowledge in these decisions the one apostolic faith of the local Churches . . . of which the bishops are the teachers (*didaskaloi*) and the guardians" (§37). The process of reception of the decisions of the bishops into the life of the churches, especially their liturgical life, is a process that involves the entire church.

Historical precedent for such a corporate understanding exists in the early church. The Acts of the Apostles reports that "the apostles and elders met together to consider the matter" (Acts 15:6) and mentions the presence of an assembly (15:12). Local synods gathered during Cyprian's time in the third-century Church of Carthage "with a multitude of faithful present" expressing their opinions.[52] At the First Ecumenical Council, laity eagerly defended the party of their choice.[53] Later, laity were displaced and represented by the Byzantine emperors and their representatives, and theologians who were not bishops participated directly or indirectly.

The conciliarity of the entire church is exercised within the liturgical assembly, the order of the assembly reflecting the order of the church. As we have seen, the ordination of baptism gives the baptized their place in the Eucharistic assembly and deputes them to participate in the official worship of the church. The priestly people are genuinely concelebrants of the Eucharist because the whole assembly, inclusive of the presider and the people, are the subjects of the liturgical action.[54] The Eucharistic worship is the corporate action of the whole church wherein every member has his or her appropriate role to perform. The anaphora is prayed in the first-person plural, "we," indicating that the priest prays on behalf of and in union with the assembly.

A synodal and conciliar church is characterized by mutual listening, mutual dialogue, mutual witnessing, and mutual respect. Ecclesial structures such as synods and councils become focal points for these activities while at the same time they exhibit the very character of the church. As St. John Chrysostom says, "Church and Synod are synonymous."[55] The ideal, as articulated in the Ravenna statement, is that there be "neither passivity nor substitution of functions, neither negligence nor domination of anyone by another."[56] The instinct of faith (*sensus fidei*), a gift of the Holy Spirit given to all the baptized, unites all the members of the church in discerning the presence of the Spirit, the mind of Christ, and the will of the Father. This prevents a rigid separation between the teaching church and the learning church "since the flock has an instinctive ability to discern the new ways that the Lord is revealing to the Church."[57] Reception of synodal decisions and formulations ultimately relies on their instinct of faith.

With respect to this instinct of faith, Pope Francis refers to the anointing of the people of God by the Holy Spirit, making it infallible in believing:

> This means that it does not err in faith, even though it may not find words to explain that faith. The Spirit guides it in the truth and leads it to salvation. As part of his mysterious love for humanity, God furnishes the totality of the faithful with an instinct of faith—which helps them to discern what is truly of God. The presence of the Spirit gives Christians a certain connaturality with divine realities, and a wisdom which enables them to grasp those realities intuitively, even when they lack the wherewithal to give them precise expression.[58]

This "sense of the faith" as a kind of "spiritual instinct" allows the people of God "to think with the Church" (*sentire cum ecclesia*) and "to discern what conforms to the Apostolic faith and to the spirit of the Gospel."[59] While not to be confused with the sociological reality of majority opinion, the principle means that "to think with the Church," one must listen to the people of God who are that church. When asked what *sentire cum ecclesia* [to think and to feel with the church] means to him, Pope Francis answered with the image of the church from *Lumen Gentium* 12, the holy, faithful people of God: "The people themselves are the subject. And the church is the people of God on the journey through history with joys and sorrows. *Sentire cum Ecclesia*, therefore, is my way of being a part of this people."[60] He then developed the infallibility in believing through a supernatural sense of the faith of all the people walking together. His "thinking with the church" involves a dialogue among the people and the bishops and the pope. For him, "this church with which we should be thinking and feeling is the home of all, not a small chapel that can only hold a small group of select people."[61] "Thinking with the church," then, involves the whole people of God and is an intrinsic component of the conciliarity of the church.

BENEFITS OF A BAPTISMAL ECCLESIOLOGY

A baptismal ecclesiology offers a beneficial corrective to several difficult issues when considering the place of the laity in the church. First, an inclusive view of the church offers a critique of clericalism and a corresponding clergy–laity divide.[62] "Clericalism" refers to the process by which an office in the church forms in church ministers the consciousness of being a privileged class or elite, with claims to recognition, symbolic boundaries to defend, and a position to secure. In contrast, a dialogical relationship between clerics or designated office-holders and the rest of the Christian faithful emphasizes the equality of the Christian faithful across a variety of charisms, ministries, and positions within the ecclesial body. Within such a context, ordination to clerical status should not be viewed as an "elevation" in status, but as a designation to a certain relationship within the body for service to the body.

Second, baptism grounds the principle and practice of conciliarity. The Ravenna statement describes conciliarity as "signifying that each member of the Body of Christ, by virtue of baptism, has his or her place and proper responsibility in eucharistic koinonia (*communio* in Latin)."[63] Each member "has a charism, a service or a proper ministry, necessary in their variety and diversity for the edification of all in the one ecclesial Body of Christ (cf. 1 Cor 12, 4–30)."[64] Furthermore, "by virtue of Baptism and Confirmation (Chrismation) each member of the Church exercises a form of authority in the Body of Christ."[65] The participation of the non-ordained in councils, the consultation of the faithful in matters of discipline and faith, and attention to the reception of doctrinal definitions so that they become embedded in the life, worship, and teaching of the church, all shift the center of gravity in the church from ordained ministers to the church as a whole. Participation in ecclesial life becomes an extension of full, active participation in the liturgy on the part of all of the baptized.

Third, this view makes it clear that the identity of the hierarchical ministry derives from its location, defined by mutual relationships within the body of all the baptized. This is to say that the identity and theology of ministry derives from the character of the church, not vice versa. Thus, as Pope Francis suggests, rather than envisioning the church as a pyramid with the hierarchy at the top and the rest of the baptized on the bottom tier, it is better to envision it as an inverted pyramid, with the ordained ministers serving the others.[66] In the important 2015 address at the fiftieth anniversary celebration of the Synod of Bishops, he used this same image, saying,

> those who exercise authority are called "minister," because, in the original meaning of the word, they are the least of all. It is in serving the people of God that each bishop becomes, for that portion of the flock entrusted to him, *vicarius Christi*, the vicar of that Jesus who at the Last Supper bent down to wash the feet of the Apostles (cf. Jn 12:1–15). And in a similar perspective, the Successor of Peter is nothing else if not the *servus servorum Dei*.[67]

Pope Francis suggested to a delegation from the Patriarch of Constantinople that "a careful examination of how, in the Church's life, the principle of synodality and the service of the one who presides are articulated, will make a significant contribution to the progress of relations between our Churches."[68] It will do this by restoring the identity and theology of the Christian faithful as a positive rather than as a remainder concept, by subordinating a theology of ministry to a theology of the church, and by contributing to ecumenical discussion of the universal ministry of the papacy by situating that discussion within reenvisioned ecclesial relationships. In this view, there cannot be a clericalism whereby those who are ordained are regarded as superior to other members; a democratization that does not sufficiently appreciate the ordained ministry itself; or a professionalization which regards as the responsibility of certain individuals those tasks that properly belong to all the people of God.

Fourth, when correlating a theology of the baptismal priesthood with that priesthood's participation in the Eucharist and when correlating ecclesiology with liturgy, it becomes evident that the concept of hierarchy is best understood liturgically. The clergy are not intrinsically above or separate from the body of believers. Since the early second century, ordained office in the local community has been trifold: a single bishop ("overseer," "supervisor"), with two sets of coworkers: a body of presbyters ("elders"), who support and advise the bishop, and a group of deacons ("ministers," "delegates"), who carry out sacramental and charitable work among the people. All these officials are ordained for service to enable the whole church to live out its distinctive role of priesthood in the world. The intimate relationship between the clergy and the rest of the Christian faithful is most clearly expressed when the church gathers to celebrate the Eucharist. Ecclesial relationships mirror liturgical relationships. Full, active participation of the entire assembly in the liturgy corresponds to the structure and life of a participative church wherein all the members speak with their own voice. This is not a democratic, but a liturgical principle. Such participation does not negate role differentiation in the church as a whole any more than it does within the liturgy, but it signals the desirability of a more inclusive role for non-ordained members in the church.

Fifth, this view enables us to see that the whole church is called to be engaged in mission. The people of God as a whole are sent into the world as the "light of the world and the salt of the earth" (cf. Mt 5:13–16). The relationship between the church and the world is perhaps best described as an interpenetration insofar as the church shares the world's earthy lot, even while it serves as a leaven within human society, renewing it in Christ and working to transform it in conformity with the kingdom of God. In this way all become apostles, the "yeast leavening the whole dough" (1 Cor 4:6). All the baptized serve as agents of evangelization, which cannot then be seen as a matter for the professionals while the rest of the faithful remain passive.

Sixth, as developed earlier, a baptismal ecclesiology recovers a robust theology of the priesthood of the baptized, and through its theology of charism and the *sensus fidei* of this priesthood makes more explicit the role of the Holy Spirit in the life of the church.

Finally, while this last point cannot be developed in this present work, a baptismal ecclesiology is helpful ecumenically in that it provides a middle ground between full ecclesial communion and no communion at all. Mutual recognition of baptism is the sacramental foundation for an imperfect communion between ecclesial communities.

CONCLUSION

The entire body of the faithful shares in various ways Christ's' triple office: as priest, as prophet (teacher, witness), and as king (servant, leader). The whole church shares in the prophetic mission of Christ in the world and shares also in his kingly role, working to advance his kingdom of justice and peace in the wider human community, offering the world the ideal of a society based on truth and love. A renewed consciousness of the mission of the church as a whole relativizes the traditional ranking of distinctive ministries and states of life, so that they are more clearly seen as contributing to a common mission and as expressing a common faith and vocation based on a common baptismal identity. From this renewed point of departure, it is clear that conciliar and synodal structures and processes must be developed to include increased participation by all the members of the church, so that these structures and processes may better reflect the composition of the church as a whole in all its variety.

Note: An earlier version of this chapter first appeared as *"Christifideles* within a Baptismal Ecclesiology: Reframing the Question of Participation in Leadership and Mission," *Studia Canonica* 58 (2024): 79–101.

NOTES

1. Walter Kasper, *The Catholic Church: Nature, Reality and Mission* (New York: Bloomsbury T&T Clark, 2015), 122.
2. Greek from σύν (*sún*, "with") (English *syn-*) + ὁδός (*hodós*, "way, path").
3. Bruno Forte, *Laïcat et laïcité* (Paris: Méduaspaul, 1986), 116.
4. Ibid.
5. Second Vatican Council, Decree on the Church's Missionary Activity, *Ad Gentes*, December 7, 1965, §2, in *Vatican Council II: The Basic Sixteen Documents*, ed. Austin Flannery, OP (New York: Costello Publishing Co., 1996). Hereafter *AG*.
6. Christian Initiation, General Introduction, §4, in *The Rites of the Catholic Church as Revised by the Second Vatican Council*, vol. 1 (New York: Pueblo, 1990), 4. Hereafter *The Rites*.
7. *The Rites*, Baptism for Children, §62.
8. Eusebius, *Historica Ecclesiastica*, I, 3, in *Patrologiae Cursus completeus. Series Graeca* (Paris: Migne, 1857–1912), vol. 20, cc. 68–73. Hereafter *PG*.
9. St. Irenaeus of Lyons, *Against Heresies*, 4.8.3. English translation: *St. Irenaeus of Lyons: Against the Heresies books 4 and 5*, trans., notes, and commentary by Scott D. Moringiello and Dominic Unger (New York: Paulist, 2024), ebook pages 49–52.
10. St. John Chrysostom, in *2 Cor homilia 3:5* in *PG*, vol. 61, 411.
11. Augustine, *In Luc.* 5:33 (Commentary on Luke 5:33), in *Patrologia Latina. Series Latina* (Paris: Migne, 1844–1864), 15.1645 (hereafter *PL*). In the *City of God* Augustine commented, "This clearly does not mean only the bishops and presbyters, who are now called by the distinctive names of 'priests' in the Church; but just as we call all Christians 'Christs' in virtue of their sacramental anointing (*chrisma*) so we call them all 'priests' because they are members of the one Priest. And the apostle Peter says of them that they are 'a holy people, a royal priesthood'" (*De civitate Dei*, 20:10, in *PL* 41.676). English translation: Augustine, *City of God* (Middlesex, England: Pelican Books, 1972), 919.
12. Fastidius, *De Vita Christiana*, 1, in *PL*, vol. 50, c. 394.
13. Peter J. Drilling, "The Priest, Prophet, and King Trilogy: Elements of Its Meaning in *Lumen Gentium* and for Today," *Église et Théologie* 19 (1988): 179–206. For histories of this trilogy see Yves Congar, "Sur la trilogie: Prophète-Roi-Prêtre," *Revue des Sciences Philosophiques et Religieuses* 67 (1983): 97–115; and L. Schick, *Das Dreifache Amt Christi und der Kirche. Zur Entstehung und Entwicklung der Trilogien* (Europäische Hochschulschriften, Reihe XXIII Theologie Bd. 171) (Frankfurt/M.—Ber, Peter Lang, 1982).

14. See the *Apostolic Tradition* attributed to Hippolytus of Rome, 21. The laying on of hands occurs in the rite of chrismation, which for the Orthodox is inseparable from baptism, both rites representing baptism by water and the Spirit (Jn 3:5). Nicholas Afanasiev, *The Church of the Holy Spirit* (South Bend, IN: University of Notre Dame Press, 2007), 24; John Zizioulas, *Being as Communion* (Crestwood, NY: St. Vladimir's Press, 1997), 216.

15. Afanasiev, *Church of the Holy Spirit*, 24; Zizioulas, *Being as Communion*, 216.

16. Zizioulas, *Being as Communion*, 216. Even though Zizioulas, in identifying baptism as an ordination to an "ordo" within the Christian community, reflects an Orthodox insight shared with Afanasiev, there are problems with his emphasis on an ecclesial hypostasis created by baptism constitutive of personhood. This appears to relegate those who are not baptized to a state of non-personhood. This also creates a kind of exclusivism with regard to non-Christians who are not seen to be in communion with the Catholic faithful.

17. Ibid.

18. Afanasiev, *Church of the Holy Spirit*, 137.

19. Ibid., 25. It is not entirely clear whether Afanasiev definitively identifies the laity with the *laos* in the manner precluded by de la Potterie's etymological study.

20. Ibid., 30.

21. Ibid., 31.

22. Ibid.

23. Ibid., 24. Presidency, however, is more than a charism. It is also an ordo within the community and a sacrament that Catholics say confers a sacramental character distinct from that of baptism.

24. Ibid., 137.

25. See Richard R. Gaillardetz, "The Ecclesiological Foundations of Ministry within an Ordered Communion," in *Ordering the Baptismal Priesthood*, ed. Susan K. Wood (Collegeville, MN: Liturgical Press, 2003), 26–51; *Ecclesiology for a Global Church* (Maryknoll, NY: Orbis, 2008), 163; "The Synodal Shape of Church Ministry and Order," *Concilium* (2021): 98–108; and Susan K. Wood, "'Ordered Ministries' for a Missionary and Global Church: The Contributions of Richard R. Gaillardetz," *Ecclesiology*, 19 (2023): 280–95.

26. See Yves Congar, "The *Ecclesia* or Christian Community as a Whole Celebrates the Liturgy," in *At the Heart of Christian Worship: Liturgical Essays of Yves Congar*, trans. Paul Philibert (Collegeville, MN: Liturgical Press, 2010), 15–68.

27. *General Instruction of the Roman Missal*, March 17, 2003, http://www.vatican.va/roman_curia/congregations/ccdds/documents/rc_con_ccdds_doc_20030317_ordinamento-messale_en.html.

28. International Theological Commission, "*Sensus Fidei* in the Life of the Church," 2014, §67, https://www.vatican.va/roman_curia/congregations/cfaith/cti_documents/rc_cti_20140610_sensus-fidei_en.html#1._The_sensus_fidei_as_an_instinct_of_faith. Hereafter ITC.

29. Ibid., §72.

30. Ibid.

31. Ibid., §§43, 72.

32. John Henry Newman, *On Consulting the Faithful in Matters of Doctrine*, ed. with an introduction by John Coulson (London: Georffrey Chapman, 1961), 63. Referenced in ITC, "*Sensus Fidei* in the Life of the Church," §77.

33. ITC, "*Sensus Fidei* in the Life of the Church," §72.

34. On the equality of members, see St. John Chrysostom, *Homilies on John*, in *PG* 10.2, *PG* 59.75; *Homilies on 2 Corinthians* 18.3, in *PG* 61.527; *Homily on Ephesians* 11.1, in *PG* 62.8.

35. See Gaillardetz, "The Ecclesial Foundations of Ministry within an Ordered Communion"; and Edward P. Hahnenberg, *Ministries: A Relational Approach* (New York: Crossroad, 2003), 122–50, 176–210.

36. The instituted ministries of acolyte, lector, and catechist will be discussed in chapter 3.

37. Synod of Bishops, *Lineamenta*: "Vocation and Mission of the Laity in the Church and in the World Twenty Years after the Second Vatican Council" (Washington, DC: US Catholic Conference, 1985).

38. John Paul II, Apostolic Exhortation, *Christifideles Laici*, On the Vocation and the Mission of the Lay Faithful in the Church and in the World, December 20, 1988, https://www.vatican.va/content/john-paul-ii/en/apost_exhortations/documents/hf_jp-ii_exh_30121988_christifideles-laici.html. Hereafter *CL*.

39. *LG* 31 identifies the laity as leaven, as does *Apostolicam Actuositatem* 2 (Second Vatican Council, Decree on the Apostolate of the Laity, *Apostolicam Actuositatem*, November 18, 1965, in *Vatican Council II: The Basic Sixteen Documents*, ed. Austin Flannery, OP (New York: Costello Publishing Co., 1996) (hereafter *AA*), but the whole church is called to fill this function.

40. Paul VI, Talk to the Members of the Secular Institutes (February 2, 1971) in *Acta Apostolicae Sedis* (AAS) 62 (1972), 208, cited by John Paul II in *CL* 15.

41. Henri de Lubac, *A Brief Catechesis on Nature and Grace* (San Francisco: Ignatius Press, 1984), 85.

42. Ibid., 43.

43. Ibid., 81.

44. Second Vatican Council, *Presbyterorum ordinis*, December 7, 1965, §2, in *Vatican Council II: The Basic Sixteen Documents*, ed. Austin Flannery (New York: Costello Publishing Co., 1996).

45. See also *LG* 9.

46. Irenaeus, *Against Heresies*, 1.9.4, *PG* 7.545; *LG* 12.

47. Joint International Commission for the Theological Dialogue between the Roman Catholic Church and the Orthodox Church, "Ecclesiological and Canonical Consequences of the Sacramental Nature of the Church: Ecclesial Communion, Conciliarity and Authority," Ravenna, October 12, 2007, §5, http://www.christianunity.va/content/unitacristiani/en/dialoghi/sezione-orientale/chiese-ortodosse-di-tradizione-bizantina/commissione-mista-internazionale-per-il-dialogo-teologico-tra-la/documenti-di-dialogo/testo-in-inglese.html. Hereafter Ravenna.

48. Ibid., §§10, 17.

49. Joseph Komonchak, "Theological Perspectives on the Exercise of Synodality in the Church," in *A cinquant'anni dall' Apostolica sollicitudo Il Sinodo dei Vescovi al servizio di una Chiesa sinodale* (Rome: Libreria editrice Vaticana, 2016), 252.

50. Ibid.
51. St. Basil the Great, *On the Holy Spirit*, 45. See https://www.documentacathol icaomnia.eu/03d/0330-0379,_Basilius_Magnus,_Liber_de_Spiritu_Sancto_[Schaff], _EN.pdf.
52. Cyprian, Epistle, 13:31, in *PL* 4.267, 309, 320, cited by John N. Karmiris, *The Status and Ministry of the Laity in the Orthodox Church* (Brookline, MA: Holy Cross, 1994), 14.
53. Socrates, *Ecclesiastical History*, 1.8, in *PG* 67.64, referenced by Karmiris, *Status and Ministry of the Laity*, 14.
54. St. John Chrysostom, *Homily on Philippians* 3.4, in *PG* 62.204. See also Nicholas Kabasilas, *Commentary on the Divine Liturgy* 1ff, in *PG* 150.369ff; and Theodoretos, *Homily on 2 Corinthians* 2.20, in *PG* 82.384.
55. St. John Chrysostom, *Explicatio in Ps.* 149.
56. Ibid., §21.
57. Francis, Address at the Ceremony Commemorating the 50th Anniversary of the Institution of the Synod of Bishops, October 17, 2015, http://w2.vatican.va/content/francesco/en/speeches/2015/october/documents/papa-francesco_20151017_50-anniversario-sinodo.html. See also *LG* 123.
58. Francis, Apostolic Exhortation *Evangelii Gaudium*, November 24, 2013, §119, https://www.vatican.va/content/francesco/en/apost_exhortations/docments/papa-francesco_esortazione-ap_20131124_evangelii-gaudium.html. Hereafter *EG*.
59. Address of Pope Francis to Members of the International Theological Commission, December 6, 2013, https://www.vatican.va/content/francesco/en/speeches/2013/december/documents/papa-francesco_20131206_commissione-teologica.html.
60. Francis, with Antonio Spadaro, *My Door Is Always Open*, trans. Shaun Whiteside (London: Bloomsbury, 2014), 49.
61. Ibid., 51.
62. Paul Meyendorff, "Towards a Baptismal Ecclesiology," in *Liturgies in East and West: Ecumenical Relevance of Early Liturgical Development* (Acts of the International Symposium Vindobonense I, Vienna, November 17–20, 2007), ed. Hans-Jürgen Feulner (Berlin: Zurich: Lit Verlag GmbH & Do. KG Wien, 2013), 285–94.
63. Ravenna, §5.
64. Ibid., §6.
65. Ibid., §7.
66. Francis, Address to the Delegation of the Ecumenical Patriarchate of Constantinople, June 27, 2015, http://w2.vatican.va/content/francesco/en/speeches/2015/june/documents/papa-francesco_20150627_patriarcato-costantinopoli.html.
67. Francis, Address at the Ceremony Commemorating the 50th Anniversary of the Institution of the Synod of Bishops.
68. Francis, Address to the Delegation of the Ecumenical Patriarchate of Constantinople.

2

A Synodal Church as a Pilgrim Church

A synodal church is a pilgrim church situated in history which is *in via*, literally "on the way," which is to say that it has not yet arrived at its destination. Pilgrimage, however, represents more than simply a journey that the church embarks upon, even though the church has been on this journey since the Acts of the Apostles. Pilgrimage is a hermeneutical lens for interpreting the very nature of a synodal church. This interpretive lens conditions how the church engages the participation of all the baptized through synodal processes, fosters communion through its sacramental life and relationships, and continues the mission of Jesus Christ by proclaiming and enacting God's message of mercy and salvation—the hallmarks of a synodal church. Pilgrimage implies that a church transmits its tradition in a dynamic, living way. Pope Francis cites Gustav Mahler saying that "fidelity to tradition does not consist in worshiping ashes but in keeping a fire burning."[1] The fire, of course, is the originating fire and power of the Gospel message that the disciples proclaimed, each in their own language, through the gift of the Holy Spirit appearing upon them in the form of tongues of flame (Acts 2:3–4). In journeying, the past is not abandoned or left behind, but the originating fire of the Gospel message is kept alive by the church being in motion and expressing and living that Gospel in changing and ever-new circumstances in various languages and cultures. Pope Francis compares the journey of the church to Vincent of Lérins's description of the development of the church's tradition, who said that the deposit of faith cannot be preserved unless it advances in such a way as "to be consolidated by years, enlarged by time, refined by age."[2] Like water, which "unless it keeps flowing, it becomes stagnant and putrefies," a stagnant church starts to decay.³ Consequently, to be faithful to its past the church must be a pilgrim, adapting and learning as it proclaims the Gospel in diversified ways to various people in various times and cultures, on its way to its eschatological fulfillment.

The identity of the church as a pilgrim is consistent across the documents of the Second Vatican Council. Pope John XXIII introduced the theme in his opening address to the council on October 11, 1962, juxtaposing the human person composed of body and soul with his status as pilgrim on this earth yet tending always toward heaven.⁴ The pilgrim is in the world, encounters and interacts with the world, witnesses to the world, but is only a sojourner in this strange and foreign land before reaching his or her final home. Nevertheless, as André Brouillette notes, "the earth is the place in which the Pilgrim Church accomplishes her mission" and therefore is "not a place to escape from."⁵ The world is the place where the Gospel is preached, where one becomes sanctified, where the reign of God comes to establish justice and right relationships, and where the Word was enfleshed, thereby bestowing dignity on all flesh.

Lumen Gentium explicitly identifies the new people of God as a pilgrim church (*LG* 13). Chapters 2 and 7 of *Lumen Gentium* both pick up on the theme of a pilgrim church and function as bookends of the document if you consider chapter 1 on the mystery of the church as an introduction and chapter 8 on Mary as a conclusion. These positions in no way detract from their importance, but on the contrary bestow even greater significance on them, the first chapter presenting the very nature of the church and the last recapitulating or embodying the church in Mary in terms of her discipleship.

Chapter 2, on the people of God, identifies the church as a messianic people whose destiny is the kingdom of God (*LG* 9). Chapter 7 describes the journey toward that destiny. However, even the first chapter describes the church as being on "the path of penance and renewal" and as pressing forward on that path "like a stranger in a foreign land . . . announcing the cross and death of the Lord until he comes" (*LG* 8). In the journey the pilgrim experiences trials and persecutions, proclaims the cross and death of the Lord until he comes again, and is thereby transformed into an image of Christ by means of the journey and its processes of growth, purification, and sanctification. The pattern is paschal: from shadows to light, from sorrow to eternal happiness, from death to life, from bondage to freedom, from exile to heavenly home. The difficulties and resulting suffering are formative for the pilgrim, potentially producing endurance, character, and hope (Rom 5:3–5). Just as the Israelites who journeyed for forty years through the desert—a journey that could have been much shorter—murmured and complained but were ultimately strengthened in their corporate identity as God's people, so too, the new people of God are formed and perfected on their journey.

Sacrosanctum Concilium, the Constitution on the Liturgy, describes the church as a "migrant, so constituted that in it the human is directed toward and subordinated to the divine, the visible to the invisible, action to contemplation, and this present world to that city yet to come, the object of our quest (see Heb 13:14)" (*SC* 2).[6] *Unitatis Redintegratio,* the Decree on Ecumenism, describes the church "like a standard lifted on high for all the nations to see, ministers the Gospel of peace to all humankind, as it makes its pilgrim way in hope towards its goal, the homeland above" (*UR* 2).[7] *Dignitatis Humanae,* the Declaration on Religious Liberty, confesses that "although, in the life of the people of God in its pilgrimage, through the vicissitudes of human history, there have at times appeared patterns of behavior which was not in keeping with the spirit of the Gospel and were even opposed to it" (*DH* 12).[8] Yet, even in the midst of these failings, "it has always remained the teaching of the church that no one is to be coerced into believing" (*DH* 12). Finally, *Dei Verbum,* the Dogmatic Constitution on Divine Revelation, compares tradition and scripture to a mirror "in which the church, during its pilgrim journey here on earth, contemplates God, from whom it receives everything, until such time as it is brought to him face to face as he really is (see Jn 3:2)" (*DV* 7).[9] It is precisely in its identification as the people of God that the church understands itself as located in history, journeying toward its eschatological fulfillment in Christ (Eph 1:10; Col 1:20). On its journey, the pilgrim church is a sign, a sort of sacrament of the ultimate communion between God and humankind (*LG* 1), a witness to the nations.

The *Synthesis Report* of the first session of the Synod on Synodality presents synodality as a pilgrimage or journey in various ways: "as a joint journey of the people of God and as a fruitful dialogue between the charisms and ministries at the service of the coming of the Kingdom;"[10] "as Christians walking in communion with Christ toward the Kingdom along with the whole of humanity;"[11] and as "a synodal journey."[12] Formation for a synodal church is undertaken synodally as the entire people of God are "formed together as they journey together."[13]

DESTINATION AND MISSION

On one level, a destination seems to designate the endpoint of a journey. While the journey of a pilgrim church might appear to be linear, aimed toward a specific destination, in this case its final and definitive union with God at the end of history, destination also can refer to the purpose of the journey in terms of mission, the reason why the journey is undertaken in the first place. This purpose is achieved not simply at the end of the journey but is enacted throughout the course of the journey, even though the mission is achieved in fullness only at the end of the journey.

As the North American final document for the continental stage of the 2021–2024 Synod states, "synodality is inseparable from becoming a Church sent forth on mission."[14] Likewise, *A Synodal Church in Mission: Synthesis Report* affirms that "synodality is ordered to mission."[15] It is often repeated that the church does not have a mission; it is a mission, for it has its origin in the mission of the Son and the Holy Spirit (*AG* 2). All the disciples of Jesus have a responsibility for mission according to their different charisms, vocations, roles, and functions. Pope Francis's Apostolic Exhortation, *Evangelii Gaudium*, contributes to a missionary transformation of the world by emphasizing the role of each member of the people of God.[16] This task cannot be left to the professionals or to the hierarchy, for each member is deputed by his or her baptism and confirmation "to offer others an explicit witness to the saving love of the Lord, who despite our imperfections offers us his closeness, his word and his strength, and gives meaning to our lives" (*EG* 121). They are not only disciples, but in the famous words of Pope Francis, "missionary disciples" who can say, "We have found the Messiah!" (*EG* 120). For Pope Francis, "mission is a constant stimulus not to remain mired in mediocrity but to continue growing" (*EG* 121). This is precisely the synodal way of a pilgrim church on a path toward continual transformation. Yet, there is but one mission, that of proclaiming Jesus Christ to the world with his saving message of the mercy of God.

Pilgrims share a common goal or destination. Traditional language labels this destination as "heaven" or "the kingdom of God." Theological language speaks of "eschatological fulfillment," the completion of all at the end time. Biblical language, more emotionally evocative and picturesque, describes it as the "new heavens and the new earth in which righteousness is at home" (1 Pt 3:13), as the new Jerusalem compared to a bride adorned for her husband, where God dwells with his people and wipes "every tear from their eyes," and where "death will be no more; mourning and crying and pain will be no more" (Rv 21: 1–4). The destination is a place of hope, newness, life, joy, restoration, and companionship and filiation with God. This vision of heaven is dynamic, not static, a place of right relationships and justice.

The destiny of the pilgrim church is inseparable from its mission and identity as "the universal sacrament of salvation" (*LG* 48, *GS* 45). As *Gaudium et Spes,* the Pastoral Constitution on the Church in the Modern World, states, "Whether it aids the world or whether it benefits from it, the church has but one sole purpose—that the kingdom of God may come and the salvation of the human race may be accomplished" (*GS* 45).[17]

As a sort of sacrament (*veluti sacramentum*, LG 1), the church—as both a sign and an effective means of grace—through its life, teaching, and worship serves to enable the people of God to live their lives in holiness, increase their faith, and be in communion with God and with each other. The church both manifests and actualizes the mystery of God's love for humanity (*GS* 45). The destiny of the whole human race is salvation, not envisioned as a static state, but rather a dynamic life of communion and right relationship with God and others as the form of salvation. The goal and destiny of human history is none other than the establishment of the reign of God in Jesus Christ, the Word of God, the alpha and omega, the beginning and end of history, in whom and animated by his Spirit all things in heaven and earth are united in him in his union with the Father (Rv 22:12–13; Eph 1:10).

Eschatology, the theology of "last things," traditionally concerned itself with death, judgment, heaven, hell, the return of Christ, and revelations about the end of time. Contemporary theology, however, emphasizes the unfolding of salvation history within the unfolding of human history as it moves toward its consummation of union with God. Eschatology, then, encompasses the direction and dynamic of human life, both individually and collectively, with all of creation as it is drawn by God to union with Godself.[18] The church is in motion, situated in history, and in constant development as it seeks to give witness to the Gospel to an ever-changing world.

This journey takes place between the cross and full participation in the resurrection[19] as the church makes its way through the dramatic interplay of sin and grace to its final fulfillment. The theme of pilgrim captures an "already" and "not yet" of an inaugurated eschatology that is the intersection of historical time and the fulfilled time of eschatology. Jesus Christ gives the church this eschatological identity by entering human history from eternity in the incarnation, uniting the earthly material of the cosmos to divinity, thereby bringing eternal time into the midst of historical time when he became human. Eschatology, the endpoint of the journey, imparts meaning and value to historical, temporal realities in light of their ultimate purpose and goal. The theme of pilgrim expresses the historical nature of the church, its provisional status as a creature *in via*—on the way—its continual need for reform and purification, its continual growth in deepening its understanding of the word of God, and its missional responsibility to work for justice in history. *Lumen Gentium* 48 expresses the intersection of these themes thus:

> Already the final age of the world is with us (see 1 Cor 10:11) and the renewal of the world is irrevocably under way; it is even now anticipated in a certain real way, for the church on earth is endowed already with a sanctity that is

true through imperfect. However, until the arrival of the new heavens and the new earth in which justice dwells (see 2 Pt 3:13) the pilgrim church, in its sacraments and institutions, which belong to this present age, carried the mark of this world which will pass, and it takes its place among the creatures which groan and until now suffer the pains of childbirth and await the revelation of the children of God (see Rom 8:19–22).

THE JOURNEY

The journey of the pilgrim church occurs within the world, which in all its materiality becomes the place of encounter with the divine, the place where "God reaches us with His saving love . . . not only at an interior level (or morally), but it reaches us in our very flesh, in our body."[20] This is the sacramental principle that God is present in the fleshly, the finite, and the historical and the principle of mediation whereby God works through the fleshly, the finite, and the historical. The material elements of the sacraments, as in the water of baptism or the bread and wine of the Eucharist, aptly named for the final journey of life as *viaticum*, become places of humanity's encounter with divine grace. Although this encounter is not limited to the sacraments of the church, God always encounters us in our materiality. According to St. Thomas's axiom that "that which is received is received according to the mode of the receiver,"[21] humans receive knowledge and experience another, including the divine "other," through their senses, their intelligence, and their affectivity.

Engagement with the surrounding world is an essential aspect of pilgrimage. As will be described in the following chapter, this encounter takes place through dialogue with the world, culture, and other faith traditions. A synodal church is not self-enclosed but journeys to the peripheries of society in order to engage in dialogue with all peoples in their various spiritual, social, and economic conditions and to proclaim to them God's saving mercy. The church not only welcomes people who approach it; it leaves the tent and seeks people where they are to be found.[22] Many of the people in the listening sessions for the synod noted that "the Church is at its best when walking alongside those forced to the margins of our society."[23]

The encounter with a wider world during the journey of pilgrimage leads to the discovery that God is not just found at the end of the journey but also in the world and in the encounters on the way. Brouillette cites Graham Tomlin, who writes, "A common outcome of good, healthy pilgrimage is a renewed and strengthened sense that God can in fact be found, not just in so-called 'holy places,' but anywhere."[24] The transformation that occurs within an individual and within a community is not unrelated to this broader encounter, for if God can be found anywhere and transformation occurs through encounter with the divine, then God is found in unexpected places—in darkness and suffering as well as in light and joy, in the barrios as well as in the cathedrals.

This connection between the journey and the surrounding world is perhaps best understood with an analogy with the *Spiritual Exercises* of St. Ignatius of Loyola. Jack Costello explains that the *Spiritual Exercises* is "at the heart of Jesuit spirituality because it deals with life as a journey, as a journey of transformation in relation to the moments of history. It is not simply an internal conversion, but an internal conversion in relation to what God is doing in the world."[25] The same is true of a synodal way of being church. The transformation occurs through the dialogue of fellow travelers as they speak of their experience in the church and in the world, as they discern together God's presence and work in the world and how best to engage with that. The transformation occurs within community and within the context of a world embroiled in war, pandemics, economic disparities, racism, the migration of peoples, ecological crises, ideological polarities, and political corruption. The transformation may be deeply personal, but the fruits of this grace are for this world and for its transformation into the reign of God.

TRANSFORMATION, REFORMATION, PURIFICATION

Because the church has a historical and a human dimension, it is liable to sin in its institutional dimension and in that dimension grows in holiness as it engages in a process of transformation into the image of Christ. The church, as *Lumen Gentium* reminds us, not only clasps sinners to itself, but is itself "at once holy and always in need of purification," following "constantly the path of penance and renewal" (*LG* 8). *Unitatis Redintegratio,* in associating the renewal of the church with an increase in fidelity to her own calling, reiterates the theme, emphasizing that "Christ summons the church, as she goes her pilgrim way, to that continual reformation of which she always has need, insofar as she is a human institution here on earth" (*UR* 6). Sanctity *in via*, on the way, is always imperfect. The fact that this path of renewal takes place within the communion of the people of God implies that sanctification is not a self-help enterprise, but only occurs with the assistance of God and others. It is not only an individual growing in love of God and neighbor, holiness being "perfection of charity" (*LG* 39), but also the building up of the whole people of God, the church, in holiness.

This dynamic description of a church always in need of reform counterbalances the more ahistorical and static image of the church as the Body of Christ.[26] Both images of the church are valuable, the first to situate the church within history and within the world, implying that it is capable of change and ongoing transformation conditioned by its historical context, and the second to situate the church in relationship to Christ and the Eucharist and to emphasize that Christ acts through the church in its sacraments and in the witness of its people. Both images of the church expand it beyond the institutional model that dominated ecclesiology up to Vatican II. Nevertheless, the dynamic image of people of God highlights the church's eschatological orientation, the notion of God's preferential love for his people, its situatedness in history, and its constant need for reform—all encompassed in its status as a pilgrim.

Perhaps one of the most important aspects of pilgrimage is the change and transformation that pilgrims undergo both as intrinsic to the nature of a journey that occurs over time and through different terrains, but also as a prerequisite for ultimately arriving at the destination. This change and transformation may be attributed to a change in perspective due to change in locale, encounters with others, distance from the distractions of usual routines and work, and the influence of grace. This change and transformation is nothing short of conversion, a turning from self-sufficiency, isolation, and selfishness to inter-dependence, community, and generosity. This conversion pertains not only to individuals within the church but also to the church itself as it journeys through different periods of history, encounters various cultures, and faces challenges to its life and faith.

André Brouillette, in his book on pilgrimage, asks whether transformation is a necessary characteristic of pilgrimage.[27] He suggests that transformation does indeed differentiate pilgrimage from other forms of travel but situates the critical moment of transformation in the return home, especially in its aftermath. The danger is that the trip itself become a parenthesis in the stream of life that limits its impact on what follows. One example he cites is World Youth Day, an event that can have significant emotional impact at the time, but which may not have long-lasting consequences. One might also add the example of the *Spiritual Exercises* of St. Ignatius of Loyola, a thirty-day retreat that Jesuits make at least twice in their lifetime, once in the novitiate and then again as part of their tertianship, the last phase of Jesuit formation. The Jesuit General Congregation 36 stated that "the question that confronts the Society today is why the Exercises do not change us as deeply as we would hope. What elements in our lives, works, or lifestyles hinder our ability to let God's gracious mercy transform us?"[28] The answer seems to lie in the need for a more robust appropriation of the *Exercises* after having experienced them. The same may be said of any religious experience, whether that be a pilgrimage, World Youth Day, or a retreat experience. Those experiences need to spill over into daily life and into commitment to others.

Ongoing reform is essential for a church on pilgrimage if it is to avoid fidelity to a particular cultural form or transitional form of the church becoming an infidelity or an obstacle to its fundamental mission. Yves Congar identifies this mission as enabling people to encounter God, stating,

> The church has not achieved what it was created to do until, at a level deeper than its conduct, its catechesis, and its institutions, it has actually led souls to a personal contact with God. When its sacramentality, its rites, and its symbols become themselves the content of what is sought and celebrated, then the church becomes an *obstacle* instead of a *means* to life with God.[29]

To serve this mission of encounter, the church is called to adapt its structures and ways of doing things for this purpose. Ecclesial structures do not exist for themselves in a kind of ecclesial introversion but exist to serve evangelization and to promote the church's fidelity to her vocation to mission. Thus, as I've previously written, "any renewal of structures that pastoral conversion demands must aim to make those structures more mission-oriented and to make pastoral activity on every level more inclusive and open."[30] Pope Francis describes this ecclesial renewal as a "missionary option," defined as "a missionary impulse capable of transforming everything, so that the Church's customs, ways of doing things, times and schedules, language and structures can be suitably channeled for the evangelization of today's world rather than for her self-preservation" (*EG* 27).

Historically, the church has experienced waves of reform movements. Notable among them was the Gregorian Reform of the eleventh century that promoted the moral integrity and independence of the clergy by prohibiting lay investiture to church office; by prohibiting simony, the practice of purchases of ecclesiastical offices; and by reinforcing clerical celibacy, not always observed among the lower ranks of the clergy although forbidden by the Council of Nicaea in 324 AD. The Council of Trent (1545–1563), the Catholic Church's reform movement in response to the Protestant Reformation, defined Catholic doctrine in reply to disputed points on the part of Protestants. These included issues such as the doctrine of justification, the relationship between scripture and tradition, the number and nature of the sacraments, the veneration of saints and relics, purgatory, and the authority of the pope. It also issued decrees of self-reform such as granting a greater authority for bishops but also requiring them to reside in their dioceses, reforming abuses such as the sale of indulgences, and improving the education of priests through the establishment of seminaries.

The Second Vatican Council (1961–1965) is the most recent ecumenical council to initiate reforms. The reforms most immediately obvious to the person in the pew were the liturgical reforms, for the council mandated that both "texts and rites should be ordered so as to express more clearly the holy things which they signify," so that the Christian people could "be able to understand them easily and take part in them in a celebration which is full, active and the community's own" (*SC* 21). Consequently, the rites of all the sacraments were revised after the council, sacred scripture was incorporated into all the sacramental rites, and an abundance of selections of scriptural texts were made available. The lectionary was revised and provided cycles of readings for the liturgical year. The participation of the people was encouraged by means of acclamations, responses, psalms, antiphons, and hymns. The use of the vernacular in the Mass and the sacraments further enhanced the understanding and conscious participation of the faithful.

Other highlights of the Vatican II reform, beyond the liturgy, include the prioritization of a more personalistic account of revelation over a propositional one in its identification of Jesus Christ as "both the mediator and the sum total of revelation" (*DV* 2). The council gave a larger role to laypeople in the church, identifying the source of their apostolate in their baptism and confirmation (*LG* 33). It affirmed the concept of religious freedom (*DH* 2), unequivocally opened the way to ecumenical and interreligious dialogue,[31] and developed the theology of the episcopacy, emphasizing its collegial nature and identifying episcopal ordination as the fullness of the sacrament of Orders (*LG* 21). In the Pastoral Constitution on the Church in the Modern World, the only document issuing from the council that originated during the council itself, the council addresses the whole of humanity, offering an analysis of the condition of the world today by "reading the signs of the time and interpreting them in the light of the Gospel" (*GS* 4) and describing the dignity of the human person and his and her individual and social roles. The council then addresses urgent problems such as the dignity of marriage and the family, the proper development of culture, economic, and social life, the political community, and peace and a community of nations.[32]

Clearly, in these documents the pilgrim church was taking an account of its environs on its journey, clearing the way to facilitate encounters with other Christians, non-Christians, and the contemporary world as it abandoned the self-isolating posture assumed in its opposition to Modernism in the late nineteenth century and entered into dialogue with the modern world. The council was responding to changed historical circumstances in a world caught up in a cold war between East and West and on the brink of annihilation with the October Missile Crisis of 1962 while still living in the atomic age inaugurated at Hiroshima and navigating the aftermath of Hitler's aggression and the Holocaust.[33]

Not all church reform awaits an ecumenical council, as a cursory review of some of the reforms of the last three pontificates shows. The contributions of John Paul II (1978–2005) are so extensive as to practically defy summary. In addition to numerous encyclicals contributing to the development of fundamental theology, the social teaching of the church, and moral theology, he contributed to church reform when he promulgated a new *Catechism of the Catholic Church* and penned one of the most important ecumenical documents, *Ut Unum sint* (1995), in which he invited ecumenical partners to help rethink the practice of the office of the papacy, perhaps the most significant barrier to Christian unity. His apostolic exhortations signaled an increased attention to the globalization of the church: *Ecclesia in Africa* (1995), *Une Espérance Nouvelle Pour le Liban* (1997), *Ecclesia in Asia* (1999), *Ecclesia in America* (1999), *Ecclesia in Oceania* (2001) and *Ecclesia in Europa* (2003). He took up the theme of evangelization and the church's mission *ad gentes*, to the nations, in *Redemptoris missio* (1990), *Tertio millennio adveniente* (1994), and *Novo millennio ineunte* (2001). He popularized the term *new evangelization*, first used by Paul VI in his 1975 apostolic exhortation *Evangelii nuntiandi*, referring to the re-evangelization of Christian people as well as mission to new regions and cultures.

Benedict XVI (2005–2013) worked to reawaken Christianity in a secularized Europe, work signalled by his chosen papal name "Benedict" after the monk, St. Benedict of Norcia (ca. 480–547), founder of the Benedictine order, credited with preserving learning and literature in Western Europe following the fall of the Roman Empire. He established the Pontifical Council for Promoting the New Evangelization and convened the Synod of Bishops on the New Evangelization for the Transmission of the Christian Faith in 2012. The apostolic constitution that followed that synod was Francis's *Evangelii Gaudium* (2013), which laid out the program of Francis's pontificate. Benedict's trilogy of encyclicals on the theological virtues of love (*Deus Caritas Est*, 2005), hope (*Spes Salvi*, 2007), and faith responded to philosophical and secularist challenges to the faith.[34]

Adopting generally conservative views after the student uprisings in 1968, Benedict attempted to counter increased Western secularization by advocating a return to fundamental Christian values. For example, his Motu Proprio *Summorum Pontificum* (2007) removed various sanctions against the use of the Tridentine Rite of the Mass. His apostolic constitution *Anglicanorum Coetibus* (2009) provided for the establishment of Personal Ordinariates for Anglicans entering into full communion with the Catholic Church, enabling them to retain their liturgical rites.

Just as Pope Benedict's chosen name signaled his agenda for his pontificate, so too did Jorge Bergolio's choice of the name "Francis." From the moment that Pope Francis announced his name after the papal election, it became clear that the reform of the church would mark his pontificate. Christ instructed Francis of Assisi, "Repair my church," and Pope Francis would attempt to do just that. The reform initiated by Pope Francis began with his emphasis on the priority of baptism and the call of all Christians to be missionary disciples. One month after his election he formed an international Council of Cardinals to advise him on governance. He opened the instituted ministries of lector and acolyte to both men and women[35] and established a new instituted ministry of catechist, also open to women and men.[36] With the document *Praedicate Evangelium* (2022), he reformed the structure of the Curia with a focus on evangelization, expanded roles for lay women and men in top leadership positions, and eliminated the previous distinction between congregations and councils, giving them all the title of "dicastery."[37]

Initiating a financial reform, Francis restructured the way money is managed in the Vatican, expanding the work of Pope Benedict XVI to monitor transactions, standardize budgeting procedures, and ensure that the Vatican bank and other financial entities are not being used for illegal activity or money laundering. He established the Council for the Economy in 2014, a group of eight cardinals and bishops and seven lay experts "to consider policies and practices and to prepare and analyze reports on the economic-administrative activities of the Holy See." He then established the Secretariat for the Economy that reported to the Council for the Economy, and that had authority over economic and administrative activities within the Holy See and Vatican City State, including a review of financial reports.[38]

Pope Francis issued two documents on liturgical reform, *Traditionis Custodes* (2021), which limits the use of the pre–Vatican II liturgy and thereby adjusts the trajectory on this issue taken by his papal predecessor,[39] and a letter on liturgical formation titled *Desiderio desideravi* (2022), that reaffirms the reformed liturgy of the Second Vatican Council while at the same time calling for a spiritual renewal with respect to the liturgy.[40] Additional contributions to liturgical reform include his section on the homily in *Evangelii Gaudium* (135–44). For Francis, "the homily is the touchstone for judging a pastor's closeness and ability to communicate to his people" (*EG* 125). The importance of the homily, which for Francis surpasses all forms of catechesis, lies within the dialogic character of the liturgical proclamation of the word of God as a moment of "dialogue between God and his people" (*EG* 137).

Clearly, as this cursory survey of conciliar and papal reforms shows, the entire history of the Catholic Church has been one of change, transformation, and reform in response to changing historical circumstances, challenges to the faith, and the need to proclaim the faith convincingly to the culture of the time.

DISCERNING AUTHENTIC REFORM

A pilgrim church must also be a discerning church as it navigates the polarities of good and evil, altruism and self-interest, and sin and grace in its engagement with the world. At any moment in history, it must discern whether a particular reform contributes to its mission or detracts from it, which is to ask, "Does any particular reform lead to a more effective proclamation of the Gospel, or not?" A church on pilgrimage may discover that reforms needed in one time or context are not suitable for another context. Discernment is especially needed in the contemporary transition from a classicist paradigm of the concept of an ordered and static world—that some might identify with an unchanging church—with its over-arching master narratives of meaning to a historicist paradigm characterized by change, multiplicity, and complexity.[41] This shift, described by Bernard Lonergan, contrasts an abstract, ahistorical perspective with a concrete, historical perspective that emphasizes the historically situated character of life, the responsibility of human beings as participants in a living tradition to actually make history and thereby form themselves as human beings "individually responsible for their lives and collectively responsible for the world in which they live."[42] A historical worldview that begins with concrete realities rather than ideas requires discernment to determine what is of God and how the church can best proclaim and live the Gospel in a particular time and place. This emphasis on concrete realities reflects Yves Congar's conviction that true renewal in the church begins with the pastoral reality of the church as it is and "aims to serve its development in charity."[43] A false reform, on the other hand, adopts "an intellectual and critical attitude that takes its point of departure from a representation of ideas and develops into a system that seeks to reform the existing reality under the influence of this system."[44] The first begins with the concrete pastoral reality, while the second begins with an idea.

This remarkably prefigures Pope Francis's statement forty-five years later in *Evangelii Gaudium*: "Realities are more important than ideas" (*EG* 231). This is but an application of the incarnational principle that the word became flesh and is "constantly striving to take flesh anew" (*EG* 233). Those things that mask reality include: "angelic forms of purity, dictatorships of relativism, empty rhetoric, objectives more ideal than real, brands of ahistorical fundamentalism, ethical systems bereft of kindness, intellectual discourse bereft of wisdom" (*EG* 231). Ideas must always serve communication, understanding, and praxis.

Both the pastoral magisterium of Pope Francis and doctrine applied pastorally have as their starting point concrete experience rather than abstract doctrine. The church is not simply the arena in which doctrines are applied, but as John O'Brien has observed, "the very context from which doctrines emerge, the very condition of possibility of doctrine and the prior and posterior praxis which doctrine, at most, attempts to sum up, safeguard, and transmit."[45] Doctrines arise from the existential experience of the faith in response to questions posed, disputes over interpretation, and the lived experience of the faith. No church council has ever attempted a complete systematic exposition of the faith, but invariably responds to a particular historical context and the needs of the church at a particular time. Moreover, doctrines never exhaust the fundamental Christian message.

A synodal church, through its practices of discernment, first listens to the Gospel to see how it addresses the signs of the time and the world in this time and in the places where it finds itself and then communally responds in the light of its mission to proclaim and enact the Gospel, whether in the mainstream of civilization or at its peripheries for the transformation of the world into the reign of God. As the evangelizers become the evangelized, so too, the church in working for the conversion of the world itself undergoes conversion in terms of how it understands and carries out its mission. It does not possess all the answers which it then dispenses, but in humility discovers them, either for the first time or anew, as it journeys with the people of God.

Doctrines are not disembodied ideas but serve the core Christian proclamation of the Gospel within the pastoral life of the church.[46] As such, they are subject to development. This change illustrates that the church's teaching must always be in touch with the reality of lived experience and the wisdom of accumulated reflection upon that experience. Core beliefs remain, and church teaching is always in continuity with its apostolic past, but the pastorality of doctrine means that doctrine is lived before it is codified, that it is not simply didactic, informative, and regulative, but doxological, mystagogical, and transformative—something to be lived when connected with its roots in the faith experience of the community.[47] Because of the transcendent nature of the church, its beliefs, and the sacred realities for which it is the custodian, the church more easily defines what a thing is not, what the church is not, and to define against error than to affirm what a thing is, what the church is, and to give a complete and exhaustive account of the faith of the church. It can never adequately give "an adequate positive expression of what it is and of everything it carries within itself."[48] Thus, for example, the first chapter of *Lumen*

Gentium does not define the mystery of the church but gives multiple images of the church such as sheepfold, God's building, house of God, new Jerusalem, spotless spouse, and so on (*LG* 6).

One example of the development of doctrine influenced by changing circumstances is the change in the teaching of the death penalty in the *Catechism of Catholic Church*. The 1992 catechism recognized "the right and duty of legitimate public authority to punish malefactors by means of penalties commensurate with the gravity of the crime, not excluding, in cases of extreme gravity, the death penalty." The 1997 update of the catechism strengthened John Paul II's skepticism about the need to use the death penalty today and affirmed the need to protect all human life, stating, "the cases in which the execution of the offender is an absolute necessity 'are very rare, if not practically nonexistent.'"[49] This section was again revised by Pope Francis so that the *Catechism* as of 2018 now states that "the Church teaches, in the light of the Gospel, that 'the death penalty is inadmissible because it is an attack on the inviolability and dignity of the human person,' and the Catholic Church works with determination for its abolition worldwide."[50]

Such development and rootedness in concrete reality is to be expected from a synodal church "on the way." A pilgrim church on the way to its perfection in charity and sanctity and to its definitive union with the Father in and through Christ in the power of the Spirit threads its way within history, adapting as it meets various challenges to achieve its mission of embodying and proclaiming God's mercy to all those on the journey.

JOURNEYING IN COMMUNION WITH OTHERS

Another condition for true church reform is that the reformer and the reform "remain in communion with the whole church."[51] Communion is both a historical communion between Christ and his people within history and a vertical communion transcending history, for "communion as participation in the Divine Life is the grounding reality of all Christian life and, therefore, of a synodal Church."[52] This reflects the nature of the church as a communion, described in *Lumen Gentium* as "a sign and instrument, that is, of communion with God and of the unity of the entire human race" (*LG* 1). This two-dimensional communion reflects a pilgrim church on its journey within history (the horizontal) toward its transcendent future destination (the vertical). Synodal communion is both human, a communion of all the baptized, and spiritual, a communion in grace with the divine persons. Furthermore, communion, as both a gift and task to be accomplished, is itself "a journey in which we are called to grow."[53]

Communion, mission, and participation have been the principal themes of the Synod of 2021–2024 from the beginning, the themes being interwoven with one another and mutually interpreting one another. Communion is the basis of co-responsibility in mission, and mission, in turn, indicates the dynamism of a pilgrim church en route to its destination, which the 2023 *Instrumentum Laboris* describes as the other-centeredness, hence ecstatic nature, of "a drive towards the 'ecstasy' that consists in 'coming out of ourselves and seeking the good of others, even to the sacrifice of our lives.'"[54] A synodal church does not exist for its own self-preservation, nor does communion exist for the comfort of the church's members, but for mission. This mission is itself communion for "mission is not the marketing of a religious product, but the construction of a community in which relationships are a manifestation of God's love and therefore whose very life becomes a proclamation."[55] Thus, rightly understood as outward-directed, communion is mission and mission is communion.

A synodal church renews its instruments of communion to enhance communion, mission, and participation in the church. The first of these is liturgical prayer. In the Eucharist particularly, the church experiences a radical unity amid a diversity of languages and rites within the liturgical sign and action that it endeavors to live out in the concrete, historical particularities of a fragmented world. What is experienced under the liturgical sign is lived out laboriously over time in the unfolding narrative of daily life. The sublimity of liturgical symbol meets the reality of the church parking lot.

Other ecclesial instruments of communion include the collegial nature of church ministry. The "orders" of ordained ministry—bishop, priest/presbyter, deacon—are all collegial bodies, reflecting the fundamentally relational character of ordained ministry. Apostolic succession is not just the ordination of an individual bishop in an apostolic line, but the entire college of bishops as a body succeeds to the college of apostles (*LG* 19). The college of bishops, a permanent assembly that a bishop enters into by episcopal ordination and hierarchical communion with the bishop of Rome, parallels the communion of particular churches that constitute the Catholic Church, with each residential bishop representing his church within that communion. The bishop oversees the unity and communion of his particular church in a way analogous to how the pope in his Petrine ministry serves the unity of faith and communion of the church. Ministers at every level of the church serve the communion of that segment of the church within itself and its communion with other levels such as parish to diocese, diocese to the church universal.

Reforms, to be effective, require widespread participation and the support of the community. Reception of church reforms, not unlike reception of doctrine, becomes part and parcel of the practical life of the church in its doctrine, life, and worship of the church (*DV* 8). Thus, the maxim from Roman law invoked since the Middle Ages now reinterpreted synodally is: *Quod omnes tangit, ab omnibus tractari debet* (Whatever affects everyone ought to be examined [treated] by everyone).[56] If synodality means that the whole church is a subject, then everyone in the church is a subject and is called upon to play an active role.[57] This principle does not negate the distinction between "making a decision" and "taking a decision." A group may make a decision or formulate a recommendation based on a discernment (making a decision), but the ratification of this decision (taking a decision) lies with a competent authority empowered to take a decision, whether this be the pope at a worldwide synod, a bishop in his diocese, a pastor in his parish, or the superior of a religious community.[58]

Finally, not only is the church a communion within itself, but it also enters into "solidarity with other religions, convictions and cultures."[59] It does this by avoiding two dangers: "the risk of self-referentiality and self-preservation" and the "risk of loss of identity."[60] The first danger is antithetical to mission and the second, to the ability to proclaim and witness to what it has experienced in its encounter with Jesus Christ. Dialogue becomes the medium of this encounter as well as service to those in need and collaboration in shared efforts for peace, justice, care for the earth, and human rights. Recognition of our shared human dignity provides basis for this solidarity as well as the church's mission to establish communion.

CONCLUSION

This chapter has traced the contours of a pilgrim church in terms of its destination and mission, demonstrating that in the very act of journeying in this historically conditioned and material world, the church encounters the divine. The journey is one of growth, purification, reformation, and transformation, enabling the church to reach "the unity of faith and of the knowledge of the Son of God, to maturity, to the measure of the full stature of Christ" (Eph 4:13). A cursory survey of church reform showed that change and reform have been constant hallmarks of the church throughout its history. Along the way, the church discerns the direction of its growth much as the vine dresser assesses the direction of growth of the vine and takes stock of whether its message of the saving mercy of God is communicated so that it can be received within the culture of the time. Finally, communion was seen to be an essential characteristic of a pilgrim church, both in the requirement to maintain communion with the church and also as inherent to its mission and structure.

NOTES

1. Francis, "We Are Church Together," Address to the Faithful of the Diocese of Rome, September 18, 2021, in Dicastery for Communication, *Walking Together: The Way of Synodality* (Maryknoll, NY: Orbis, 2023), 151–63, at 157.

2. Vincent of Lérins, *Commonitorium primum*, 23, (*ut annis consolidetur, dilatetur tempore, sublimetur aetate*), cited in Francis, "We Are Church Together," 157.

3. Ibid.

4. John XXIII, "Pope John's Opening Speech to the Council," October 11, 1962, in *The Documents of Vatican II*, ed. Walter M. Abbott, SJ (New York: America Press, 1966), 714.

5. André Brouillette, *The Pilgrim Paradigm: Faith in Motion* (New York: Paulist, 2021), 157.

6. Vatican II, "Constitution on the Liturgy, *Sacrosanctum Concilium*, December 4, 1963," in *Vatican Council II: The Basic Sixteen Documents*, ed. Austin Flannery, OP (New York: Costello Publishing Co., 1996). Hereafter *SC*.

7. Second Vatican Council, "Decree on Ecumenism, *Unitatis Redintegratio*, November 21, 1964," in *Vatican Council II: The Basic Sixteen Documents*, ed. Austin Flannery (New York: Costello Publishing Co., 1996). Hereafter *UR*.

8. Second Vatican Council, "Declaration on Religious Liberty, *Dignitatis Humanae*, December 7, 1965," in *Vatican Council II: The Basic Sixteen Documents*, ed. Austin Flannery (New York: Costello Publishing Co., 1996). Hereafter *DH*.

9. Second Vatican Council, "Dogmatic Constitution on Divine Revelation, *Dei Verbum*, November 18, 1965," in *Vatican Council II: The Basic Sixteen Documents*, ed. Austin Flannery (New York: Costello Publishing Co., 1996). Hereafter *DV*.

10. Secretaria Generalis Synodi, XVI, Ordinary General Assembly of the Synod of Bishops, First Session, October 4–29, 2023, Vatican City, "Introduction," *A Synodal Church in Mission: Synthesis Report*, https://www.usccb.org/resources/2023.10.28-ENG-Synthesis-Report_IMP.pdf.

11. Ibid., I. 1. Convergences, h.

12. Ibid., I. 2. b.

13. Ibid., III. 14. f.

14. North American Final Document for the Continental Stage of the 2021–2024 Synod, "For a Synodal Church: Communion, Participation, and Mission," October 2022, §35, https://www.usccb.org/resources/North%20American%20Final%20Document%20-%20English.pdf.

15. *A Synodal Church in Mission: Synthesis Report*, chapter 8.

16. Francis, Apostolic Exhortation *Evangelii Gaudium*, §§119–22, November 23, 2013, https://www.vatican.va/content/francesco/en/apost_exhortations/documents/papa-francesco_esortazione-ap_20131124_evangelii-gaudium.html. Hereafter *EG*.

17. Second Vatican Council, "Pastoral Constitution on the Church in the Modern World, *Gaudium et Spes*, December 7, 1965," in *Vatican Council II: The Basic Sixteen Documents*, ed. Austin Flannery (New York: Costello Publishing Co., 1996). Hereafter *GS*.

18. Gerard Mannion, "The Pilgrim Church: An Ongoing Journey of Ecclesial Renewal and Reform," in *The Cambridge Companion to Vatican II*, ed. Richard R. Gaillardetz (Cambridge: Cambridge University Press, 2020), 115–35, at 116.

19. Walter Kasper, *The Catholic Church*, 122.

20. Commission on Spirituality Sub-Group: Spirituality for Synodality, "Towards a Spirituality for Synodality," Synod 2021–2023, 16. https://www.usccb.org/resources/Spirituality-of-Synodality-A4-Orizzontale-EN.pdf.

21. "*Quidquid recipitur ad modum recipientis recipitur.*" See Thomas Aquinas, *Summa Theologiae*, vol. 11 (New York: Blackfriars, 1970) for 1a, q. 75, a. 5; and vol. 48 (New York: Blackfriars, 1976) for 3a, q. 5.

22. North American Final Document, "For a Synodal Church: Communion Participation and Mission," §54.

23. Ibid., §33.

24. Brouillette, *Pilgrim Paradigm*, 44, citing Graham Tomlin, "Protestants and Pilgrimage," in *Explorations in a Christian Theology of Pilgrimage*, ed. Craig Bartholomew and Fred Hughes (Hants: Ashgate, 2004), 122.

25. Jack Costello, SJ, interview for "The Jesuit Mystique," *Ideas*, CBC Radio One, writer and researcher Michael W Higgins, producer Bernie Lucht, 1994–1995, cited in Michael W. Higgins, *The Jesuit Disruptor: A Personal Portrait of Pope Francis* (Toronto: House of Anansi Press, 2024), 66.

26. See Pius XII, Encyclical, *Mystici Corporis*, June 29, 1943, https://www.vatican.va/content/pius-xii/en/encyclicals/documents/hf_p-xii_enc_29061943_mystici-corporis-christi.html.

27. Brouillette, *Pilgrim Paradigm*, 43.

28. Society of Jesus, General Congregation 36, d. 1, no. 18 (Society of Jesus, 2017), https://jesuits.eu/images/docs/GC_36_Documents.pdf.

29. Yves Congar, *True and False Reform in the Church*, trans. Paul Philibert (Collegeville MN: Liturgical Press, 2022), 129. Original: *Vraie et fausse réforme dans l'Église*, rev. (Paris: Cerf, 1968). See also Avery Dulles, "True and False Reform," *First Things* 135 (2003): 14–19.

30. Susan K. Wood, SCL, "Francis's Church Reform Focused on the Proclamation of Mercy: The Ignatian Influence," *Studies in the Spirituality of Jesuits* 55, no. 3 (2023): 1–45, at 36.

31. Second Vatican Council, Declaration on the Relation of the Church to Non-Christian Religions, *Nostra Aetate*, 28 October 1965, in *Vatican Council II: The Basic Sixteen Documents*, ed. Austin Flannery (New York: Costello Publishing Co., 1996). Hereafter *NA*.

32. *Gaudium et Spes*, 1–5.

33. For the historical context of the council, see Stephen Schloesser, SJ, "Against Forgetting: Memory, History, Vatican II," *Theological Studies* 67 (2006): 275–319.

34. The last was begun by Benedict, but completed by Francis and issued as *Lumen Fidei* in 2013.

35. Francis, Apostolic letter Motu Proprio, *Spiritus Domini*, January 10, 2021, https://www.vatican.va/content/francesco/en/motu_proprio/documents/papa-francesco-motu-proprio-20210110_spiritus-domini.html.

36. Francis, Apostolic letter Motu Proprio, *Antiquum Ministerium,* May 10, 2021, https://www.vatican.va/content/francesco/en/motu_proprio/documents/papa-francesco-motu-proprio-20210510_antiquum-ministerium.html.

37. Francis, Apostolic letter *Desiderio Desideravi,* June 29, 2022, https://www.vatican.va/content/francesco/en/apost_letters/documents/20220629-lettera-ap-desiderio-desideravi.html.

38. Francis, Apostolic Letter Motu Proprio, "On the Limits and Modalities of Ordinary Administration," January 6, 2024, https://www.vatican.va/content/francesco/en/apost_letters/documents/20240116-lettera-ap-amministrazione.html.

39. Francis, Apostolic Letter Motu Proprio, *Traditionis Custodes* (On the Use of the Roman Liturgy Prior to the Reform of 1970), July 16, 2021, https://www.vatican.va/content/francesco/en/motu_proprio/documents/20210716-motu-proprio-traditionis-custodes.html.

40. Francis, *Desiderio Desideravi.*

41. Bernard Lonergan, "Dimensions of Meaning," in *Collected Works of Bernard Lonergan,* vol. 4, ed. Frederick E. Crowe and Robert M. Doran (Toronto: University of Toronto Press, 1988), 245.

42. Bernard Lonergan, "Existenz and aggiornamento," in *Collected Works of Bernard Lonergan,* vol. 4, ed. Frederick E. Crowe and Robert M. Doran (Toronto: University of Toronto Press, 1988), 229.

43. Ibid., 227.

44. Ibid.

45. John O'Brien, "Ecclesiology as Narrative," *Ecclesiology* 4 (2008): 148–65, at 150.

46. See Wood, "Francis's Church Reform Focused on the Proclamation of Mercy," 26.

47. See Juan Louis Segundo, *The Liberation of Dogma: Faith, Revelation, and Dogmatic Teaching Authority,* trans. Philip Berryman (Maryknoll, NY: Orbis, 1992), 108.

48. Congar, *True and False Reform,* 231.

49. See John Paul II, Encyclical *Evangelium Vitae,* March 25, 1995, §9, https://www.vatican.va/content/john-paul-ii/en/encyclicals/documents/hf_jp-ii_enc_25031995_evangelium-vitae.html.

50. *Catechism of the Catholic Church,* §2267. See "New Revision of Number 2267 of the *Catechism of the Catholic Church* on the Death Penalty—Rescriptum "Ex Audientia SS.MI," October 13, 2017, https://www.vatican.va/roman_curia/congregations/cfaith/ladaria-ferrer/documents/rc_con_cfaith_doc_20180801_catechismo-penadimorte_en.html; and Congregation for the Doctrine of the Faith, "Letter to the Bishops Regarding the New Revision of Number 2267 of the Catechism of the Catholic Church on the Death Penalty," August 1, 2018, https://www.vatican.va/roman_curia/congregations/cfaith/ladaria-ferrer/documents/rc_con_cfaith_doc_20180801_lettera-vescovi-penadimorte_en.html.

51. Congar, *True and False Reform,* 229.

52. Commission on Spirituality Sub-Group, "Towards a Spirituality for Synodality," 13.

53. XVI Ordinary General Assembly of the Synod of Bishops, "For a Synodal Church: Communion, Participation, Mission," *Instrumentum Laboris* for the First

Session (October 2023), B. 1., §46, https://www.synod.va/content/dam/synod/common/phases/universal-stage/il/ENG_INSTRUMENTUM-LABORIS.pdf. Hereafter *IL*, First Session.

54. *IL*, First Session, §51. Here the document refers to the etymology of the word "ecstatic," meaning "to stand out from."

55. Ibid., §52.

56. Congar, *True and False Reform*, 241.

57. International Theological Commission, *Synodality in the Life and Mission of the Church*, March 2, 2018, §55, https://www.vatican.va/roman_curia/congregations/cfaith/cti_documents/rc_cti_20180302_sinodalita_en.html. Hereafter ITC.

58. *IL*, First Session, §69.

59. *IL* First Session, *A Synodal Church in Mission: Synthesis Report*, 2.

60. Ibid.

3

Diversity within a Synodal Church

A synodal church is necessarily a diversified church, which must always be considered in light of the mission of the church. Diversity does not exist for diversity's sake. Nor is a more decentralized church more desirable than a heavily centralized one because of some kind of postmodern suspicion of authority. As the *Instrumentum Laboris* for the second session of the Synod on Synodality explains, "Just as there is no mission without context, there is no Church which is not rooted in a given place, with its particular culture and unique history."[1] Different times and different contexts require different structures, possibly different ministries, and different formation initiatives. Both diversity and a greater decentralization exist to accomplish the mission of the contemporary church.

One description of the church's mission is found in *Apostolicam Actuositatem*, the Decree on the Apostolate of Lay People:

> The work of Christ's redemption concerns essentially the salvation of men and women; it takes in also, however, the renewal of the whole temporal order. The mission of the church, consequently, is not only to bring people the message and grace of Christ but also to permeate and improve the whole range of temporal things. (*AA* 5)

The mission is twofold. The first part of the mission concerns grace and the final destination of the pilgrim people as communion with God. The second, characterized by the term "temporal order," refers to everything in our human history. This text can be interpreted within the relationship between nature and grace such that the mission of the church is about people's relationship to God and their eternal destiny, but that it is also about grace permeating the temporal order so that it is renewed and becomes the new creation.

To accomplish this mission, the church must reach people in their specific existential realities, for it is there that they live out in their daily lives the universal call to holiness which is nothing more or less than a perfection of charity (*LG* 40). Secondly, if the church is "to permeate and improve the whole range of temporal things," this is only accomplished in concrete circumstances, institutions, and historical contexts. As the *Instrumentum Laboris* for the Second Session of the Synod of Bishops (2024) states, the missionary synodal life of the church proceeds from the perspective of places "that are the tangible contexts for our embodied relationships, marked by their variety, plurality and interconnection, and rooted in the foundation of the profession of faith, resisting human temptations to abstract universalism."[2] Neither salvation nor "the whole range of temporal things" are general.

An ecclesiology for a synodal, pilgrim church focused as it is on the reality of the church as it is instantiated in various regions and cultures, is necessarily contextual and inductive. The ecclesial community on pilgrimage is a communion of diversity rather than a monochromatic, one-dimensional, uniform community. It is a differentiated communion made up of various races, cultures, ages, states of life, vocations, charisms, and talents. In addition, the church journeys through different historical times, navigates different political and economic environments, and finds itself embroiled in different ideological conflicts. Many different points of view contribute to and sometimes compete within the symphonic complexity that is the church, much as harmonies and dissonances complement one another in creating a multilayered, rich fabric of sound. As with music, the ear must listen for and discern the subtle and not-so-subtle interplay of these harmonies and dissonances.

A synodal church listening to the voices of the people of God places an emphasis on the local church from the bottom up in order to create communion and encourage participation directed toward mission.[3] This means that the church does not have one cultural expression, especially a Roman one, which is one cultural expression among many, as the Eastern churches in communion with the church of Rome have long shown. Francis, citing John Paul II, writes, "The history of the Church shows that Christianity does not have simply one cultural expression, but rather, 'remaining completely true to itself, with unswerving fidelity to the proclamation of the Gospel and the tradition of the Church, it will also reflect the different faces of the cultures and peoples in which it is received and takes root.'"[4] As both Amanda Osheim and Natalia M. Imperatori-Lee have pointed out, this kind of decentered, localized approach "allows ecclesiology to avoid the marginalization of nondominant voices and reveals, in some sense, the invariable core of the Christian message in all its various cultural, historical, and linguistic expressions."[5] This aligns with Francis's desire for the church "to reach all the 'peripheries' in need of the light of the Gospel" (*EG* 20).

Two concepts, "globalization" and "*mondialisation*," both borrowed from the economic world to describe the production and exchange of goods, may help us to think about how different entities within the church, most often local churches, relate to one another within different models of communion. "Globalization" is different from the French "*mondialisation*" (literally translated as "worldwide-ization"), although only the word "globalization" exists in English. The two terms must be distinguished to understand why and how diversity and decentralization in the church contribute to the mission of the church today.[6]

"Globalization" implies the dissolution of national identities and the abolishment of borders inside the world network of exchanges and the emancipation of capitalism from national financial regulation.[7] It represents a kind of totalization. Globalization flattens difference and erases individual identities in the interest of free trade. In globalization, there is an apparent homogeneity or unity, even though this appearance may conceal imbalances of power.[8] That one can go almost anywhere in the world and find the same fast-food franchises is an example of globalization.

"*Mondialisation*," according to Derrida, resides in a Euro-Christian *nexus* of meaning. It differs from globalization in that it

> gestures towards a history, it has a memory that distinguishes it from that of the globe, of the universe, of Earth . . . For the world begins by designating, and tends to remain, in an Abrahamic tradition (Judeo-Christian-Islamic but predominantly Christian), a particular space-time, a certain oriented history of human brotherhood, of what in a Pauline language . . . one calls *citizens of the world* . . . brothers, fellow men, neighbors, insofar as they are creatures and sons of God.[9]

Mondialisation, then, incorporates a sense of history with its correlative notion of *telos* or destination, both of which correspond to a Christian notion of history and an ecclesiology of a pilgrim church. The notion of "worldwide" allows for particular differences that "global" does not.

Victor Li argues, however, that the concept of *mondialisation* offers a deconstruction of Anglo-American "globalization" in terms of its "ethico-politico-juridical concepts of national sovereignty and territory, cosmopolitanism, human rights, and international law" by leading them back to their European and Judeo-Christian filiation.[10] In effect, this unveils globalization, revealing it to be "Europeanization" emanating from a Christian Europe.[11] According to Li, this disrobes globalization of its cloak of any claim to cultural neutrality, revealing a hegemony of Christian

Europe resulting in a *mondialisation* that is really a "*mondialatinization.*"[12] Here, he identifies neutrality, seen as an objective, non-biased distance where only market forces prevail, as a characteristic of globalization. *Mondialisation*, however, is not unbiased because it is culturally embedded in values and particular belief systems. Nevertheless, at this point, *mondialatinization* appears to be a form of globalization insofar as elements of the Latin church are transposed to other cultures, analogous to how fast-food franchises are multiplied around the globe. At any rate, it shares characteristics of both globalization in the universalizing of some of its historical forms such as a common liturgy, use of Latin, and canon law and of *mondialisation* in that it represents one cultural form of Christianity, a Roman one.

One could argue that *mondialatinization* is what resulted from the church's missionary efforts that accompanied the colonialization of non-Christian lands. While the church has no interest in claiming neutrality because of its commitment to faith claims, one can question whether its *mondialatinization* is really a subset of globalization, the hegemony of one form of Christianity reproduced globally. A more varied *mondialisation*, though, has always been present in the life of the church in a variety of liturgical rites, notably Eastern rites, even after the Gregorian reforms, in the Eastern code of canon law, and in the reforms of Vatican II. Francis's desire to further decentralize the church enhances that.

Globalization and *mondialisation* appear as two opposing forces, one toward homogenization and ahistorical uniformity of one culture throughout the globe, and the other toward a historically embedded diversity and plurality of cultures. The 2020s are witnessing a pushback to globalization in the form of increased nationalistic tendencies, isolationist policies, increased tariffs, and resistance to immigration. This results in increased *mondialisation,* although economic forces still militate against this because they have become unmoored from national controls and regulation.

Neither globalization nor the new political *mondialisation* provide viable models for the church. The first represents a universal culture, while the second with its isolationism erodes communion among local entities, whether they be nations or churches, even putting them in competition with one another. Nevertheless, the concept of *mondialisation* offers a model of worldwide cultural diversity as an alternative to the imposition of one global culture along the lines of globalization. The ecclesiological challenge lies in how to instantiate cultural diversity and at the same time retain a unity in fundamental identity and belief.

Communion ecclesiology supplies a model for navigating between the Scylla of globalization and the Charybdis of the new isolationist political model of *mondialisation* while showing what is necessary for a worldwide church. However, not all communion ecclesiologies operate similarly. Some models of communion ecclesiology are closer to the description of globalization presented here rather than to *mondialisation,* so one has to distinguish carefully between them. The ecclesiological key is the text from *Lumen Gentium* 23 stating that "it is in and from these [particular churches] that the one and unique catholic church exists." This text explains that the relationship between the church as a whole and individual, particular churches is one of reciprocal or mutual inclusion. This is the nature of ecclesial communion. Individual churches are neither subdivisions of a universal church, nor is the universal church a federation of particular churches. The relationship is one of co-inherence.

The church in Rome is one particular church, albeit a privileged one with whom the other particular churches must be in communion, but it is not the universal church. The universal church exists only in the communion of particular churches, not apart from them. Contrastively, a notion of communion ecclesiology that envisions communion as a common sharing of a particular cultural expression of the faith would be an example of ecclesial globalization. It also represents a highly centralized church. The *Instrumentum Laboris* for the Second Session of the Synod on Synodality reflects this relationship of *mondialisation* in its explanation that the communion of the churches "each with its local concreteness, manifests the communion of the faithful in the one and unique Church, avoiding its evaporation into an abstract and homogenizing universalism."[13]

A model of communion ecclesiology conceived as a network of particular churches in communion with one another, including the church of Rome, with structures of communion and communication, instantiating the church in specific cultures and geographic locations, represents ecclesial *mondialisation*. It is a model of a more decentralized church consisting in sharing in the essential elements of the Catholic faith and the elements essential to be a church while allowing for diverse cultural expressions of the faith in liturgy, the organization of local churches, and the ministries that serve them. This is a more decentered and diversified church, centrifugal in its missionary outreach to the peripheries. Here communion is not "union with" that becomes absorption into one form of Catholicism along the model of globalization, in this case a Roman form, but rather a "communion in diversity." The model, of course, is the Trinity, where there is a unity of substance and a plurality of persons.

One must then ask, "What makes a church local?" *Lumen Gentium* identifies a local church as "a community of the altar under the sacred ministry of the bishop" (*LG* 26), describing the church in terms of word, sacrament, and ministry. This description, although presuming a particular time, place, and persons, remains generic and non-exhaustive. It gives the elements necessary for a community to be a church, but it does not describe what is local about it. It also does not specify other necessary elements such as an apostolic rule of faith, a canon of scripture, or even baptism.[14] Joseph Komonchak, in describing what makes a local church local, emphasizes locality, particular cultures, and historicity: "an embodied appropriation of the word and grace of God in communities gathered in particular times and places and confronting specific cultural and historical challenges."[15] He notes that "the terms 'local' and 'particular' Church are also used of organically linked groups of Churches, distinct 'matrices of faith' within the unity of faith and structure, enjoying their own discipline, liturgical usages, and theological and spiritual patrimonies."[16] Komonchak's description identifies the locality of local churches as places of diversity in terms of discipline, liturgy, and history within a unity of faith and structure. This description is one of ecclesial *mondialisation*, the church existing worldwide, but exhibiting a diversity of cultural expressions.

The diversity of the church needs to be reflected in inculturated forms of ecclesial organization and ministry, for the needs of the church vary vastly from region to region as well as their readiness for change.[17] Within a model of *mondialisation*, the implementation of various ministries and ecclesial practices need not necessarily be universal. One part of the church may implement a ministry or practice apart from others. This is already the case since, for cultural reasons, many dioceses in Africa are presently not implementing *Fiducia Supplicans*, Francis's declaration allowing the blessing of individuals in irregular marriages or same-sex unions.[18] In some areas of the world catechists assume a leadership role that differs from the role of most catechists in North America. In the future, one region of the world may request and receive permission to ordain married men. Some regions may implement the permanent diaconate more than others. If women are admitted to the diaconate, here again, implementation may vary from place to place. The role of episcopal conferences in requesting change and adaptation becomes more important in a model of *mondialisation* because the conference is situated best to know the culture and context of the church in that place.

To work, a decentered church along the model of *mondialisation* requires both strong structures of communion and discernment. An ecclesial *mondialisation* avoids the isolationist version of contemporary political *mondialisation* through strong structures of communion that facilitate communication and sharing among the particular churches. Absent this communion, particular churches risk the isolation of some contemporary political and economic forms of *mondialisation*. Structures of communion range from worldwide structures to regional structures to local structures such as councils at various levels, worldwide and diocesan synods, and episcopal conferences.

This model of communion ecclesiology also requires a high degree of discernment both to determine the essential elements that must be retained and to discriminate between those cultural elements compatible with the faith and those that deviate from it. Discernment is also required to determine what is best for a particular time and place. This is a relatively new practice for ecclesial structures, one which is neither top-down decision-making nor parliamentarian power politics of forming coalitions and caucuses to make decisions by majority vote. Under Pope Francis, the church is getting a crash course in discernment, in prayerful looking for the guidance of the Holy Spirit, and in arriving at consensus.

STRUCTURES TO FACILITATE COMMUNION WITHIN DIVERSITY

The structures of communion needed for a diversified, decentered church to signify the communion among churches and to foster church unity have always existed from the beginning of the church, although some have varied depending on the historical circumstances. The New Testament bears witness to Paul's travels to the churches and exchanges of greetings and information. The Council of Jerusalem was the earliest recorded gathering to resolve a disputed question in the church, the requirement for Gentile converts to the new Christian movement. As early as 120 AD, bishops had the practice of sharing the *fermentum,* a particle of the Eucharistic bread, with the bishop of another diocese or with their local priests as a sign of the communion between the churches.

While it has been customary to consider various structures in the church according to successive levels or degrees using a pyramidal model of moving from the universal to the local or vice versa, such as from the parish to the diocese, to the episcopal conference, to the whole church, the *Instrumentum Laboris* for the Second Session reminds us that "the network of relationships and the exchange of gifts between the Churches have always been interwoven as a web of relations rather than conceived as linear in form."[19] The desire is to overcome a static notion of space that imprisons and produces pastoral redundancy and to foster interdependency among the various ecclesial entities.

One example of a static notion of place might be the traditional notion of parish boundaries defined by geography rather than a more fluid association of people joining by personal preference, although, this too, has its problems. While free association promotes parochial diversity in terms of the diversity of various parishes themselves, it risks having the like-minded associate with each other and therein lose the diversity that might otherwise exist within a particular parish. What the document had in mind, however, was more the need to evangelize those people not found in these spaces at all, like the young. The need is to bring the church and the Gospel to those places where it is absent. The goal is to have the church interact with the culture of the place where it finds itself, one that is more dynamic and mobile, outside of the confines of ecclesiastical spaces and perhaps outside of traditional parishes. The priest worker movement originating in France in the 1940s, where priests wore secular clothes and worked in factories to evangelize the working class, represents one attempt to do this. The movement was suspended in the 1950s because of the left-wing politics associated with it and a perceived abandonment of the traditional priesthood. Francis's desire to go out of the peripheries requires different models of ecclesial engagement. The church in many places cannot expect people to come to it but must go out to meet the people where they are in all their diversity in terms of cultures, traditions, and languages. The *Instrumentum Laboris* stresses that the message of salvation cannot be reduced "to a single understanding of ecclesial life and its liturgical, pastoral, or moral expression."[20]

Regardless of what structure is envisioned, whether this be a base Christian community, a parish, a diocese, or a worldwide synod—a synodal church proceeds with wide, transparent, and accountable consultation to allow for diverse voices to be heard. This gives decision-takers the information needed for informed judgments that promote the unity of the people of God. Canon law presently stipulates that if a consensus emerges, the authority should not depart from it without an overriding reason, even though a consultative opinion is not binding.[21]

While other church structures and ministries remain to be developed and implemented more widely, such as the incorporation of base community structures within parishes, the mandatory use of diocesan pastoral councils, and diocesan and regional synods, this present discussion of diversity within a synodal church will focus on worldwide synods, regional episcopal conferences, and local instituted ministries. These illustrate how established structures and ministries can be leveraged with the help of ecclesial discernment to incorporate diversity that better serves the mission of the church.

Worldwide: Synods

In addition to ecumenical councils, which are rare events in the life of the church, the Synod of Bishops is a worldwide structure that facilitates the communion of the church. The synod differs from an ecumenical council because it is composed of a comparatively small number of bishops rather than the whole episcopate and because it has been traditionally consultative rather than deliberative in its authority, making it strictly an advisory body unless the pope grants it deliberative power in certain cases. The 1983 Code of Canon Law describes the Synod of Bishops as

> a group of bishops who have been chosen from different regions of the world and meet at fixed times to foster closer unity between the Roman Pontiff and bishops, to assist the Roman Pontiff with their counsel in the preservation and growth of faith and morals and in the observance and strengthening of ecclesiastical discipline and to consider questions pertaining to the activity of the Church in the world.[22]

Paul VI, in his Motu Proprio *Apostolica Sollicitudo*, established the Synod of Bishops as a permanent institution to carry forward the conciliar experience and to assist the pope in governing the universal church.[23] His initial description received further elaboration in the *Ordo Synodi Episcoporum Celebrandae,* issued in 1966 and revised in 1969, 1971, and 2006.[24] Since then, procedures for each synod have been revised and the procedures have evolved over time. Most recently, in 2018, Pope Francis issued an Apostolic Constitution, *Episcopalis Communio*, which reshapes the synodal process in several ways: (1) by providing for the laity to send their contributions directly to the synod's secretary general; (2) by providing for the possibility of a pre-synodal meeting such as occurred for the Synod of Bishops on Young People; (3) by specifying the work that must be carried out after the synod; and (4) by specifying the authority of the final document, saying that the synod's final document, if approved by the synod members with "moral unanimity," and if the pope has granted "deliberative power to the Synod Assembly," becomes part of the Ordinary Magisterium of Catholic teaching "once it has been ratified and promulgated by him."[25]

Since 1965 there have been twenty-nine synods (fifteen ordinary synods, three extraordinary synods and eleven special synods), all of which were limited to the participation of bishops.[26] The voting participants and the way of proceeding in the Synod on Synodality (2021–2024) represents a considerable change since the first Synod of Bishops in 1967. Francis, in convoking the Synod on Synodality, modified the structure of the synod, enlarging its membership to include lay people as voting members. The method of dialogue used in the synod will be described in detail in chapter 5, but here it suffices to highlight the diversity represented in the synod. For the 2023 Synod, seventy non-bishop members participated, half of whom were women. Francis received criticism because in doing this, he used an established structure to do something new by appointing non-bishops, which raised the question of whether this assembly should still be called a "Synod of Bishops."[27] Cardinal Grech, the secretary general for the Synod on Synodality, explained at a news conference that the consultative process involving laypeople and their inclusion as voting members would not "undermine" the nature of the synod as a meeting of bishops.[28] At the 2021–2024 Synod of Bishops, 70 of the estimated 370 voting members at the opening session were non-bishops.

The new model operative for the Synod on Synodality with its diverse participants and extensive consultation responds to the gap between two kinds of consensus, an ecclesial consensus arrived at by listening to all the people of God versus an episcopal consensus of a Synod of Bishops, comprised solely of bishops.[29] The expanded participation and broad consultation allowed the consensus of bishops to be more broadly informed by an emerging consensus of the church.[30]

In doing this, Francis integrates the synod into a larger framework that Rafael Luciani describes as "one that involves all our walking *together* by reason of the co-responsibility of all the *faithful* as subjects, as well as for the evangelizing mission of the whole church."[31] In this, Francis calls upon the *sensus fidei* (sense of the faith) of the whole people of God, not just that of the bishops, and places the synod at the service of the evangelizing mission of the whole church, not just the pope.[32] As Luciani observes, this expansion of the synod does not simply represent an expansion of episcopal collegiality; it places episcopal collegiality within the context of a synodal church. This is particularly evident when one considers the preparatory work for the synod at the level of the episcopal conferences and the continental reports that contributed to the work of the synod.

Although it remains to be seen whether future worldwide synods of bishops on other topics will continue a similar methodology of inclusive participation, Francis's expansion of the synod as well as the consultation of the faithful before the synod is a mechanism for increasing the diversity of voices contributing to the discernment process and promoting broad participation. Even though earlier synods had elicited responses from episcopal conferences and other groups to *lineamenta*, the 2023–2024 Synod on Synodality initiated an extraordinary process of consultation modeling a synodal process in preparation for the synod. It began with a diocesan phase, in which all dioceses were asked to hold listening sessions to which parishioners as well as those who see themselves as outsiders to the church were welcome. The diocesan phase led to a continental phase, those contributions subsequently feeding into the Synod on Synodality. Thus, consultation was initiated at local levels to inform higher levels. The variety of materials available to the 2023 Synod included the Preparatory Document (2021): *For a Synodal Church. Communion, Participation, Mission*; reports of the local churches; the Working Document for the Continental Stage (2022): *For a Synodal Church—Communion, Participation, Mission; Enlarge the Space of Your Tent* (Is. 54:2); Final Documents of the Continental Assemblies (2023); and the *Instrumentum Laboris* (2023, 2024).[33]

An unprecedented 1.3 billion Catholics worldwide could potentially be involved. The fruits of the consultation process were forwarded to Rome from 112 out of 114 episcopal conferences and by 15 Eastern churches, forming the basis of the Working Document for the Continental Stage, *Enlarge the Space of your Tent* (Is 54:2). Seven continental stage meetings, "Ecclesial Assemblies," were organized, including participants from all levels of ecclesial life, namely bishops, priests, religious, and laity for Asia, Africa, North America, Latin America and the Caribbean, Europe, Oceania, and the Middle East. These reports then fed into the preparations for the second session in 2024 and its *Instrumentum Laboris*. Clearly, the Synod on Synodality, in its preparation, organization, and documents mobilized an unprecedented effort to be inclusive in its promotion of communion and participation for the mission of the church.

Regional: Episcopal Conferences

Episcopal conferences are regional structures whose territorial area generally follow geographical, linguistic, or national contours. Although about forty of these existed before the Second Vatican Council, the council confirmed their status as a means of meeting the needs of the region and of providing an opportunity for bishops to meet regularly to share their experience and jointly formulate programs for the common good of the church.[34] John Paul II set limits to the authority of episcopal conferences with his motu proprio, *Apostolos Suos* (1998), which states that doctrinal declarations of the conference when approved unanimously can be issued as exercises of "authentic magisterium" to which the faithful are obliged to adhere with a sense of "religious respect." Lacking unanimity, a conference cannot issue such a teaching unless a declaration receives a two-thirds majority and a *recognitio*, a recognition of approval, from the Holy See, which they will not receive unless the majority is "substantial."[35] The reason for this restriction addresses the tension between local cultural situations and communion with a larger, more diversified church, for *Apostolos Suos* states, "The *recognitio* of the Holy See serves furthermore to guarantee that, in dealing with new questions posed by the accelerated social and cultural changes characteristic of present times, the doctrinal response will favor communion and not harm it, and will rather prepare an eventual intervention of the universal magisterium."[36] Here, the emphasis is on the universal church rather than on particular cultural diversity, and it would seem that any particularity must be subsumed into a universal whole in a move toward centralization. "Communion" is not necessarily a (com)union of diverse entities, but union with an eventual universal intervention that would apply to the whole church. At that point, there would no longer be local particularity. In terms of the earlier discussion, this would be an example of globalization.

A very different notion of communion is operative in Francis's modifications of the authority of episcopal conferences. As early as 2013 he stated in *Evangelii Gaudium* that "a juridical status of episcopal conferences which would see them as subjects of specific attributions, including genuine doctrinal authority, has not yet been sufficiently elaborated. Excessive centralization, rather than proving helpful, complicates the Church's life and her missionary outreach" (*EG* 32). His efforts to empower episcopal conferences began in 2017, when he restored to them the authority "to faithfully prepare . . . approve and publish the liturgical books for the regions for which they are responsible after the confirmation of the Apostolic See."[37] The Congregation for Divine Worship and the Discipline of the Sacraments had formerly been responsible for judging the fidelity of a translation of the Latin text and to supply corrections for the translations. Francis clarified the limited authority of this congregation to confirm liturgical translation in a letter to Cardinal Robert Sarah, the prefect of the Congregation, released October 22, 2017.[38] Henceforth, it is the episcopal conferences that have the faculty to make judgments on liturgical translations, even though they may be in dialogue with the Holy See. This change attenuates the hegemony imposed by the directives for translation in *Liturgiam Authenticam*, the congregation's 2001 instruction on translation requiring word for word correspondence rather than dynamic equivalency.[39] Francis noted that a translation must not only be faithful to the original text, but also to the particular language into which it is being translated, and the text must be intelligible to the people. Francis's action was faithful to Vatican II, where *Sacrosanctum Concilium* had said that translation had to be approved "by the competent territorial ecclesiastical authority" (*SC* 35).

The ecclesiastical culture wars over liturgical language and translations are at least in part a struggle between diversity and uniformity, inculturation over a monolithic imposed culture, and particularity over universality. *Sacrosanctum Concilium* had advocated much more latitude than was imposed just prior to Francis, for its norms for liturgical adaptation state, "Even in the liturgy the church does not wish to impose a rigid uniformity in matters which do not affect the faith or the well-being of the entire community. Rather does it cultivate and foster the qualities and talents of the various races and nations" (*SC* 37). The constitution directs that provision shall be made "for legitimate variations and adaptation to different groups, regions and peoples, especially in mission countries" (*SC* 38). Practices from a people's way of life may be admitted into the liturgy if they "harmonize with its true and authentic spirit" (*SC* 37).

One example of liturgical inculturation from a Canadian context is the incorporation of indigenous smudging ceremonies into penitential rites. Smudging, a cultural ceremony using the smoke of sage, sweetgrass, or cedar, signifies cleansing of body, mind, and spirit, promoting balance and harmony. It can also be used to purify a sacred space. It was used as part of the liturgy when Francis visited Canada in July 2022 to apologize to indigenous communities for the church's participation in the efforts of residential schools to uproot them from their traditional culture. This was not such an innovation, because twenty years before, on August 1, 2002, an elderly female shaman performed a purification ritual known as a *limpia* when John Paul II celebrated Mass and the beatification of two indigenous men in Mexico City.[40]

Work on the status of episcopal conferences has proceeded steadily during Francis's pontificate. Francis discussed the status of episcopal conferences in the light of his comment in paragraph 32 of *Evangelii Gaudium*, in a meeting with the College of Cardinals on February 28, 2018.[41] The reflection was a rereading of *Apostolos Suos* in the light of the decentralization that Francis promotes. Concrete steps in this direction were taken with the publication of his apostolic constitution, *Praedicate evangelium* (2022). Although the primary objective of the document was to reform the central governing structure of the Catholic Church, the Roman Curia, Francis there identifies episcopal conferences, including their regional and continental unions, as "currently one of the most significant means of expressing and serving ecclesial communion."[42] They are a place where the communion of bishops find visible expression in service to the communion of the church, itself is a communion of particular churches, grounded in the communion of the faithful, which lies at the base of the other communions.[43] Then, in 2024, the *Instrumentum Laboris* for the Second Session of the Synod on Synodality in 2024, in recognition of the role of episcopal conferences in expressing and facilitating diversity in the church, presented the proposal for the "recognition of Episcopal Conferences as ecclesial subjects endowed with doctrinal authority, assuming socio-cultural diversity within the framework of a multifaceted Church, and favoring the appreciation of liturgical, disciplinary, theological, and spiritual expressions appropriate to different socio-cultural contexts."[44] As will be discussed below, Francis's empowerment of episcopal conferences presumes a robust process of discernment for the implementation of these diverse expressions.

Local Structures

The communion of the church finds expression in a number of ongoing local structures, what canon law refers to as "organs of communion," such as diocesan pastoral councils, presbyteral councils, and parish councils.[45] Going forward, a synodal way of being church infuses every level of the church with a methodology, a spirituality, and an ethos of inclusivity, consultation, and prayerful deliberation with which it engages its work. The occasional event of a worldwide synod becomes a paradigm for more local expressions of synodality. One might even make the case that these more local experiences of synodality are more effective in initiating and implementing needed ongoing reform in the church. As Congar noted right after the Second Vatican Council, "most of the time, initiatives do not come from the center but from the periphery—from below rather than from above," while the central organs of the church assure unity and continuity with the church's apostolic foundations.[46]

DIVERSIFIED MINISTRIES

Diversified ministries are needed to meet the pastoral needs of various regions. To cite one example, the report of the Amazon Synod noted that many Amazonian communities go for a year or more without the Eucharist and other sacraments because of a shortage of priests. It recommended that criteria be established for the priestly ordination of "suitable and esteemed men of the community who have had a fruitful permanent diaconate."[47] The bishops supported the proposal 128 to 41. Additionally, a large number of consultations in the Amazon requested that the permanent diaconate be opened to women and expressed the wish to share their experiences and reflections with the Study Commission on the Diaconate of Women that Francis had established in 2016. That proposal also overwhelmingly passed, 137 to 30.

Although Pope Francis endorsed the bishops' final document, the apostolic exhortation that followed the synod, *Querida Amazonia*, did not make any reference to married priests, but only asked for missionary clergy to be sent to the Amazon and for bishops to promote prayers for priestly vocations. The reason the pope gave for not approving the request for married priests, even though he had encouraged synods to request them if needed, was that he felt that there had not been a true discernment of the issue. In his opinion the debate had become a parliamentary-style battle between different sides. Francis said, "We must understand that the synod is more than a parliament, and in this specific case, it could not escape the dynamic. On this subject it was a rich productive and even necessary parliament; but no more than that. For me, this was decisive in the final discernment."[48]

Here, Francis is not necessarily disagreeing with the content of the request, but with the process used to arrive at it. He is not saying that his response would not change in the future, but clearly, he expects a methodology of discernment to be the basis for decision-making in episcopal conferences. A decision cannot be the result of a struggle between two ideologies or power groups where there are winners and losers. Nor can it be a decision based on a rational, abstract argument divorced from a particular historical context. In this case, it is not the general question, "On principle, should married men be ordained priests?" The decision must proceed from prayer, from a discernment of the movement of the Holy Spirit, and be a consensus with which those participating can support even if they personally disagree with it. Finally, it must be grounded in experience and the concrete realities of a given time and place and assist the church in pursuing its mission.

INSTITUTED MINISTRIES

An area of ministry that has witnessed significant changes since Vatican II and that has the potential of serving the mission and evangelizing efforts of the church in very diverse contexts is that of the instituted ministries of acolyte, lector, and catechist. As lay ministries that are more strongly vocational and stable beyond the service of occasional volunteers in the church, their authorization reenforces the character of the church as an ordered communion of a variety of ministries, both lay and ordained. The specific duties of these instituted ministries are adaptable according to the needs of a particular locale under the direction of the bishop or his delegate.

Pope Paul VI established instituted lay ministries in the church, those of lector (reader) and acolyte, with his Motu Proprio *Ministeria Quaedam* (1972), while modifying the steps leading to the ordained priesthood, suppressing first tonsure, the other minor orders, and the subdiaconate.[49] However, he reserved the lay instituted ministries of acolyte and lector to men. In making these changes, Paul VI intended that the distinction between the lay instituted ministries and sacramental orders of the diaconate, presbyterate, and episcopate would "bring out more clearly the distinction between clergy and laity, between what is proper and reserved to the clergy and what can be entrusted to the laity." However, because they were reserved to men, these instituted ministries were not widely implemented in the church apart from bestowing them on candidates for ordination as deacons and priests, for whom they were required before ordination. Although in *Ministeria Quaedam* Paul VI also offered episcopal conferences the possibility of requesting that the Apostolic See institute other ministries that the conferences might consider necessary or useful in their territories, this did not happen. Conceivably, even from this early date, it would have been possible to have a great variety of formally recognized and liturgically instituted ministries. One of the reasons why episcopal conferences and dioceses have been slow to implement instituted ministries is that these have traditionally been viewed almost exclusively as liturgical functions that could be performed by extraordinary ministers, they were restricted to men, and they were disconnected from the larger mission of the church. Another reason has been a fear of clericalizing lay ministry by giving some lay ministers special status.

Pope Francis modified the criteria for access to these ministries with his Motu Proprio *Spiritus Domini* (2021), permitting the lay instituted ministries of acolyte and lector to be entrusted to all suitable faithful, whether male or female.[50] Previously, women had been permitted to serve as readers since 1970 and as altar servers since 1994 without receiving the instituted ministries. Admitting women to the instituted ministries expands their ministry beyond their functional service within the liturgy since the instituted ministries are now envisioned as situating liturgical service within a broader participation in the mission of the church. Francis further widened the practice of instituted ministries with his Motu Proprio *Antiquum Ministerium* (2021) by creating the additional instituted ministry of catechist, to respond to the increasing awareness of the need for evangelization in the contemporary world (*EG* 163–68).[51] This action builds on work begun by Paul VI with *Ministeria quaedam*, which in addition to establishing the instituted ministries of acolyte and lector, had also named the ministry of catechist as an example of an additional ministry that conferences of bishops could request.

Instituted ministries are officially established, stable lay ministries that exercise leadership through coordinating and directing others in the community in close, mutual collaboration with the pastoral ministry of bishops, priests, and deacons. An instituted ministry is a formally recognized ecclesial ministry conferred on a baptized and confirmed individual through an officially approved liturgical rite after appropriate biblical, theological, spiritual, and pastoral formation. It is exercised in a stable, ongoing manner as contrasted with a more occasional service. It represents a vocation for the person instituted, a vocation that is discerned both by the individual and by the church. Thus, instituted ministries incorporate elements of vocational discernment, preparation and formation, education, and authorization through official ecclesial recognition and liturgical installation.

Instituted ministries offer a new way of understanding and incarnating the mission of the church, which today calls for a diversification of ministries and the engagement of all the baptized in mission. To envision the ecclesial role of instituted ministries, especially those of acolyte and lector, the guiding principle is that liturgical functions mirror ecclesial responsibilities. For example, in the early church the person who presided over the liturgy, the sacrament of unity, was the person who exercised pastoral leadership in the community.[52] The deacon's service at the altar reflects his service to the poor and needy within the community. In addition to the proclamation of the word of God in the liturgy, the lector's service of the faith may include other activities that communicate and promote the word of God, such as instructing children and adults in the faith, preparing them to receive the sacraments worthily, and bringing the message of salvation to those who have not received it.[53]

An acolyte serves not only the sacrament of the altar during the Eucharistic liturgy, but also may bring communion to the sick and the homebound. In the absence of a priest or deacon, an acolyte may publicly expose and later repose the Eucharist for the adoration of the faithful.[54] With the delegation of the local Ordinary, and under the conditions laid out by him, an instituted acolyte may lead a celebration with the distribution of Holy Communion Outside Mass in the absence of a priest or deacon, following the norms of their episcopal conference. The acolyte is also called upon to serve the communion that is the church outside of liturgical events. As the homily for the Rite of Institution exhorts the candidate for institution: "In performing your ministry, bear in mind that, as you share the one bread with your brothers and sisters, so you form one body with them. Show a sincere love for Christ's Mystical Body, God's holy people, and especially for the weak and the sick."[55]

Catechists are called to be "co-responsible in the local church for the proclamation and transmission of the faith, carrying out this role in collaboration with the ordained ministers and under their guidance." Proclamation and teaching, however, describe only a part of the ministry of instituted catechists as they are also called "to collaborate with ordained ministers in the various forms of the apostolate, carrying out many functions under the guidance of the pastors."[56] The new instituted ministry of catechists raises to a new visibility those lay people whose life's work is Christian formation and education, and it further empowers those catechists in some areas who already serve as the primary local church leaders. Although the ministry of the catechist can be expressed in multiple forms, depending on the needs of the local church and the discernment of the bishop, broadly speaking there are two profiles of catechists envisioned within this instituted ministry. The first primarily has the task of catechesis as well as a role of leadership and supervision of other people who do catechesis and sacramental preparation, to which additional responsibilities may be added at the discretion of the bishop.

The second profile includes catechists who may have the broader task of participating in different forms of apostolate and community leadership in collaboration with the ordained ministers. Such functions may include, but are not limited to, guiding community prayer, especially the Sunday liturgy in the absence of a priest or deacon; assisting the sick; leading funeral celebrations; training and guiding other catechists; coordinating pastoral initiatives; human promotion according to the church's social doctrine; helping the poor; and fostering the relationship between the community and the ordained ministers. Even in these activities the catechist functions as a lay minister, avoiding any form of clericalization.[57]

Which profile is implemented largely depends on the context and needs of the local church.[58] Local communities will vary in terms of the size of the territory, the number of ordained ministers, their pastoral organization, whether they are an established church or a comparatively new young church, and other factors. The local bishop determines the specific roles and tasks to be undertaken by the catechist without the necessity of formally determining which of the two profiles is being implemented. In every case, however, the catechist is inserted into the mission of the church to work for evangelization. The second profile of catechist requires not only the basic catechetical formation of the first profile, but also additional pastoral and leadership skills. The overlap between the potential responsibilities of different ministries in the church, as for example in an overlap among the responsibilities of deacons, lectors, and catechists, indicates a certain fluidity in pastoral organization depending on the needs and resources of a particular context.

The implementation of these new ministries implies a new vision of pastoral organization, to be understood in a co-responsible rather than in a hierarchical way. Considered as an ordered communion, the church is a network of intersecting relationships. Paul VI, in *Ministeria Quaedam*, cites the liturgical principle in the reform of the liturgy that "the very arrangement of the celebration itself makes the Church stand out as being formed in a structure of different orders and ministries."[59] Instituted ministries represent a kind of ecclesial repositioning within the people of God, a position not defined by status, but by service.

CONCLUSION

A synodal church exists to enable the church to announce the Gospel of Christ's saving mercy to various peoples, nations, and cultures. In doing this, the church is implanted in various contexts so that it may accompany the diverse people of God on their pilgrim journey to final union with God. This diversity requires a model of communion, one compared to *mondialisation* and contrasted with globalization, consisting as a network of diversity with strong bonds of communion within a unity of faith where the one church is instantiated in each particular church, each with its own language, culture, and local customs. A synodal church requires strong structures of communion to maintain unity and to serve the church in its various locales.

At the worldwide level, the 2021–2014 Synod on Synodality is an instance of a modification of the makeup and manner of the proceedings of the Synod of Bishops, expanding both participation and consultation to allow more diverse voices, especially those of marginalized people, to be heard. Episcopal conferences are regional structures naturally situated to be best in touch with the people of God in that place. They are thereby able to advocate for and to implement the ministries best able to serve them, whether that be to request the ordination of men for their local church or to employ various instituted ministries for the mission of the church.

The second major requirement for a diverse church within the model of *mondialisation* is discernment—the discernment to distinguish between that which is essential and that which may be particular to a specific context and subject to change. Discernment is also the methodology for decision-making at various levels of church polity as the conclusion of a listening process incorporating diverse voices. Chapters 5 and 6 will treat dialogue and discernment in common in detail.

Diversity is a given in today's world. A change in the style of conducting oneself as a church in a synodal way, not a change in its substance or faith, is what is needed for the new evangelization. A synodal way of proceeding enables the church to announce the Gospel convincingly in this time, to the diversity of peoples, cultures, and places in today's world.

NOTES

1. "How to Be a Missionary Synodal Church," *Instrumentum Laboris*, for the Second Session of the 16th Ordinary General Assembly of the Synod of Bishops (October 2024), July 9, 2024, §53, https://press.vatican.va/content/salastampa/en/bollettino/pubblico/2024/07/09/240709d.html. Hereafter *IL*, Second Session.

2. Introduction, *IL*, Second Session.

3. Francis, "Three Keywords: Communion, Participation, Mission," October 9, 2021, in *Walking Together: The Way of Synodality*, 167.

4. Francis, *EG* 116, citing John Paul II, *Novo Millennio Ineunte*, January 6, 2001, §40.

5. Natalia M. Imperatori-Lee, "Unsettled Accounts: Latino/a Theology and the Church in the Third Millennium," in *A Church with Open Doors: Catholic Ecclesiology for the Third Millennium*, ed. Richard R. Gaillardetz and Edward P. Hahnenberg (Collegeville, MN: Liturgical Press, 2015), 45–63, at 46, cited by Amanda C. Osheim, "Stepping toward a Synodal Church," *Theological Studies* 80, no. 2 (2019):

370–92, at 378; and Osheim, *A Ministry of Discernment: The Bishop and the Sense of the Faithful* (Collegeville, MN: Liturgical Press, 2016).

6. Since English only has one word, "globalization," to refer to both realities, I will keep the French to distinguish between globalization and *mondialisation*, cautioning readers that if they read the literature on this in translation, it is likely to reduce both to "globalization."

7. Cynthia Ghorra-Gobin, "Notion en débat: mondialisation et globalisation," *Géoconfluences*, December 2017, https://geoconfluences.ens-lyon.fr/informations-scientifiques/a-la-une/notion-a-la-une/mondialisation-globalisation. Economically and politically, globalization has been challenged by reassertions of nationalism, cancellation of trade agreements, and the imposition of tariffs.

8. Victor Li, "Elliptical Interruptions or, Why Derrida Prefers *Mondialisation* to Globalization," *New Centennial Review* 7, no. 2 (2007), 141–54, https://muse.jhu.edu/article/228232.

9. Jacques Derrida, "Globalization, Peace, and Cosmopolitanism," in *Negotiations: Interventions and Interviews 1971–2001*, ed. E. Rottenberg (Stanford, CA: Stanford University Press, 2002) 275, cited by Li, "Elliptical Interruptions," 147.

10. Li, "Elliptical Interruptions," 147.

11. Ibid., 148.

12. Ibid.

13. "How to Be a Missionary Synodal Church," *IL*, Second Session, §80.

14. Eucharistic communities in religious houses, schools, and health care facilities differ from a parish in that a parish has a baptismal font and baptizes. Thus, they do not figure in the ecclesial structure in the same way as a parish. See Susan K. Wood, "Presbyteral Identity within Parish Identity," in Susan K. Wood, ed., *Ordering the Baptismal Priesthood: Theologies of Lay and Ordained Ministry* (Collegeville, MN: Liturgical Press, 2003), 175–94, at 184–85.

15. Joseph Komonchak, "Ecclesiology of Vatican II," *Origins* 28 (April 22, 1999): 763–68, at 765.

16. Ibid.

17. Francis, Post-Synodal Apostolic Exhortation, *Querida Amazonia*, February 2, 2020, https://www.vatican.va/content/francesco/en/apost_exhortations/documents/papa-francesco_esortazione-ap_20200202_querida-amazonia.html.

18. Francis, Declaration *Fiducia Supplicans*, On the Pastoral Meaning of Blessings, December 18, 2023, https://www.vatican.va/roman_curia/congregations/cfaith/documents/rc_ddf_doc_20231218_fiducia-supplicans_en.html.

19. Ibid., §78.

20. Ibid., §81.

21. Code of Canon Law (*Codex Iuris Canonici*), Latin-English Edition (Washington, DC: Canon Law Society of America, 1983), Canon 127, §2, 2. Hereafter *CIC*.

22. *CIC* 1983, Canon 342.

23. Paul VI, Apostolic Letter Motu Proprio, *Apostolica Sollicitudo*, September 15, 1965, https://www.vatican.va/content/paul-vi/en/motu_proprio/documents/hf_p-vi_motu-proprio_19650915_apostolica-sollicitudo.html.

24. Synod of Bishops, *Ordo Synodi Episcoporum Celebrandae*, Accessed July 23, 2024, https://www.vatican.va/roman_curia/synod/documents/rc_synod_20050309_documentation-profile_en.html.

25. Francis, Apostolic Constitution, *Episcopalis Communio*, September 15, 2018, https://www.vatican.va/content/francesco/en/apost_constitutions/documents/papa-francesco_costituzione-ap_20180915_episcopalis-communio.html.

26. However, there have been non-bishop members such as major religious superiors, representatives of various ecclesial groups and movements, and theological experts (*periti*), who participated as non-voting observers.

27. See Francis, *Episcopalis Communio* 7; Art. 6.

28. Joan Frawley Desmond, "Laity Voting at the Synod of Bishops—What Would Paul VI Say?" *National Catholic Register*, May 19, 2023, https://www.ncregister.com/news/laity-voting-at-the-synod-of-bishops-what-would-paul-vi-say.

29. Osheim, "Stepping toward a Synodal Church," 383.

30. Julie Clague, "Catholics, Families, and the Synod of Bishops: Views from the Pews," *Heythop Journal* 55 (2014): 985–1008, at 988.

31. Rafael Luciani, *Synodality: A New Way of Proceeding in the Church* (New York: Paulist Press, 2022), 71.

32. The *sensus fidei* will be discussed in more detail in chapter 6.

33. These are available at the Synod 2021–2024 website: https://www.synod.va/en.html. For essays on the reports of each of the continental assemblies, see *The People of God Have Spoken: Continental Ecclesial Assemblies within the Synod on Synodality*, ed. Myriam Wijlens and Vimal Tirimanna, CSsR (Dublin: Columba Books, 2023), also available at https://www.synod.va/en/synodal-process/the-continental-stage/final_document.html.

34. Vatican II, *Christus Dominus*, October 18, 1965, 36–38, https://www.vatican.va/archive/hist_councils/ii_vatican_council/documents/vat-ii_decree_19651028_christus-dominus_en.html.

35. John Paul II, Moto Proprio, *Apostolos Suos,* May 21 ,1998, §22, https://www.vatican.va/content/john-paul-ii/en/motu_proprio/documents/hf_jp-ii_motu-proprio_22071998_apostolos-suos.html.

36. Ibid.

37. Francis, Motu Proprio, *Magnum Principium*, September 3, 2017, modifying Can. 838. https://www.vatican.va/content/francesco/en/motu_proprio/documents/papa-francesco-motu-proprio_20170903_magnum-principium.html.

38. Cindy Wooden, "In Letter to Cardinal Sarah, Pope Clarifies New Translation Norms," *Catholic News Service*, October 22, 2017, https://web.archive.org/web/20171022173538/http://www.catholicnews.com/services/englishnews/2017/in-letter-to-cardinal-sarah-pope-clarifies-new-translation-norms.cfm.

39. Congregation for Divine Worship and the Sacraments, *Liturgiam Authenticam*, March 28, 2001, https://www.vatican.va/roman_curia/congregations/ccdds/documents/rc_con_ccdds_doc_20010507_liturgiam-authenticam_en.html.

40. Reported in "La Limpia: What You Didn't Know about the Traditional Healing Ritual," Mitú, April 17, 2023, with video of the event at https://wearemitu.com/wearemitu/culture/la-limpia-traditional-healing-ritual/.

41. Briefing by the Director of the Holy See Press Office Greg Burke on the 23rd meeting of the Council of Cardinals with the Holy Father Francis, February 28, 2018, https://press.vatican.va/content/salastampa/en/bollettino/pubblico/2018/02/28/180228d.html.

42. Francis, Apostolic Constitution, *Praedicate evangelium*, March 19, 2022, §7, https://www.vatican.va/content/francesco/en/apost_constitutions/documents/20220319-costituzione-ap-praedicate-evangelium.html.

43. "The emergence of episcopal conferences in the Latin Church represents one of the more recent forms in which the *communio Episcoporum* has found expression in service to the *communio Ecclesiae* grounded in the *communio fidelium*." *Praedicate evangelium*, §7.

44. "How to Be a Missionary Synodal Church," *IL*, Second Session, §97.

45. See *CIC* 1983, Canons 460–68.

46. Congar, *True and False Reform*, 239.

47. Special Assembly of the Synod of Bishops for the Pan-Amazon Region, 6 to 27 October 2017, Final Document, "The Amazon: New Paths for the Church and for an Integral Ecology," http://secretariat.synod.va/content/sinodoamazonico/en/documents/final-document-of-the-amazon-synod.html.

48. Cited in Christopher Lamb, "Pope Reveals Why He Said 'No' to Married Priests," *The Tablet*, September 4, 2020, https://www.thetablet.co.uk/news/13334/pope-reveals-why-he-said-no-to-married-priests.

49. Paul VI, Motu Proprio *Ministeria Quaedam*, August 15, 1972, https://www.ewtn.com/catholicism/library/ministeria-quaedam-9006#.

50. Francis, *Spiritus Domini*.

51. Francis, *Antiquum Ministerium*.

52. Hervé Legrand, OP, "The Presidency of the Eucharist According to the Ancient Tradition," in *Living Bread Saving Cup: Essays on the Eucharist*, second ed., ed. R. K. Seasoltz (Collegeville, MN: Liturgical Press, 1987), 1–30.

53. See notes for the Homily for the Rite of Institution of Readers, §4, in *The Rites of the Catholic Church*, vol. 2 (Collegeville, MN: Liturgical Press, 1991), 104–5.

54. "Eucharistic Worship Outside Mass," §91, in *The Rites of the Catholic Church*, vol. 1 (Collegeville, MN: Liturgical Press, 1990), 673.

55. "Homily of the Rite of Institution of Acolytes," §4 in *Rites*, vol. 2, 107–8.

56. Congregation for Divine Worship and the Discipline of the Sacraments, Letter to the Presidents of the Episcopal Conferences on the Rite of Institution of Catechists, §11, December 3, 2021, https://www.vatican.va/roman_curia/congregations/ccdds/documents/rc_con_ccdds_doc_20211203_lettera-rito-istituzione-catechisti_en.html.

57. Francis, *Antiquum Ministerium*, §7.

58. Congregation for Divine Worship and the Discipline of the Sacraments, Letter on the Rite of Institution of Catechists, §6.

59. Paul VI, Motu Proprio *Ministeria Quaedam*, August 15, 1972, https://www.ewtn.com/catholicism/library/ministeria-quaedam-9006.

4

Spirituality for a Synodal, Pilgrim Church

Broadly understood, spirituality is what shapes our relationship to the transcendent God as revealed in Jesus Christ and our relationship to other people and to creation. It gives us our stance in the world, informs our values, and orients our vision. A spirituality for a synodal church on pilgrimage is multifaceted, beginning with sensitivity to the Holy Spirit animating and guiding the church. It is shaped and nourished by the sacramental life of the church, especially baptism and the Eucharist. For a synodal church on pilgrimage, similar to the wanderings of the Israelites in the desert, a synodal spirituality "on the way" represents a passage from bondage to freedom, enabling the church to proclaim Christ's salvific message of mercy and reconciliation in a wounded world. Finally, a synodal church embodies humility, in imitation of the humble Christ, so that it may accompany and deeply listen to those it seeks to serve.

When on a pilgrimage, initial enthusiasm and motivation for undertaking the journey needs to be sustained for the long haul by returning to the reason for undertaking the journey in the first place and by keeping the destination in view.[1] As applied to the church, this would entail returning to the founding inspiration of the early disciples in their encounters with the earthly Jesus and the experience of the early church as recounted in the scriptures. The destination of the journey is union with God, with and through the assistance of one another. Salvation is communion with Father, Son, and Spirit in communion with all others enfolded in that embrace. As *Lumen Gentium* expresses the communal nature of salvation, God has "willed to make women and men holy and to save them, not as individuals without any bond between them, but rather to make them into a people who might acknowledge him and serve him in holiness" (*LG* 9). With the motivation and the destination in mind, spiritual freedom governs how the church proceeds on its way. The things of the earth are to be used and enjoyed to the extent that they contribute to this end and avoided to the extent that they are obstacles to that end.[2] The point is to be free from attachments—which for the church may be structures, customs, or the careerism of its leaders—that obstruct this purpose and mission. The goal is to be nimble and to travel light so to be able to follow where Christ leads.

A PNEUMATOLOGICAL SPIRITUALITY

A spirituality for a synodal pilgrim church is necessarily grounded in the presence and work of the Holy Spirit. As André Brouillette observes, "The Spirit breeds movement. . . . Her biblical images suggest evanescence and power associated with primal elements of nature: fire, wind, breath."[3] She is the connection of love between the Father and Son within the dynamic interrelationship of the three divine persons within the Trinity and enables the faithful to cry out, "Abba, Father" (Rom 8:15–16).[4] A pneumatological spirituality is essentially God dwelling within us, with his power and his love. As an alternate prayer for the entrance antiphon for Pentecost Sunday drawn from Romans 5:5 proclaims, "The love of God has been poured into our hearts through the Spirit of God dwelling within us." The Spirit dwells in the hearts of the people of God, not only individually but also collectively, as in a temple (1 Cor 3:16). Like the embers in a hearth at the center of a home, the Spirit dwells in the hearts of the faithful and is the spark of divine love and the source of apostolic zeal that impels them to proclaim and live the Gospel.

The fire of love of the Spirit is a creative force for renewal, reformation, and purification. The church prays in the Gospel Acclamation for Pentecost, "Come, Holy Spirit, fill the hearts of your faithful and kindle in them the fire of your love." And the response of Catholics for generations from Psalm 104 has been, "Send forth your Spirit and they shall be created, and you shall renew the face of the earth." In the power of the Spirit the people of God experience God's love in their lives and share it with others. The dynamism of the fire of the Spirit empowers the dynamism of the church on the move as it goes out to the peripheries to engage in mission rather than self-protection and self-preservation.

A synodal church celebrates and prays for the continual descent of the Holy Spirit upon each person, dwelling in their hearts as in a temple (*LG* 12), to bestow different "charisms (gifts of grace) and ministries (forms of service in the Church in view of her mission)"[5] to rejuvenate and constantly renew the church. This diversity of gifts originated at Pentecost when the Holy Spirit descended upon the disciples in forms of tongues of fire who then "began to speak in other languages, as the Spirit gave them ability" and the crowd heard them "speaking in the native language of each" (Acts 2:4, 6). The Spirit who descended upon the disciples in the form of tongues of flame now "speaks by means of the tongue of every person who lets himself be guided by God," an essential attribute of a synodal church.[6] This diversity contributes to the church as an ordered communion of various ministries and states of life that function within and contribute to an overarching unity, having its foundation in the diversity within unity of the divine life of the Trinity and in a common baptism.

The "freshness of the Gospel" that Pope Francis suggests as a solution to current problems is only possible with the help of the Holy Spirit. What is needed is a return to evangelical zeal even more than the reform of structures, organizations, and administration.[7] Thus, in *Evangelii Gaudium* Francis exclaims, "God save us from a worldly Church with superficial spiritual and pastoral trappings! This stifling worldliness can only be healed by breathing in the pure air of the Holy Spirit who frees us from self-centeredness cloaked in an outward religiosity bereft of God. Let us not allow ourselves to be robbed of the Gospel" (*EG* 97). This revitalization of the church is both the work of the Spirit and a sign that the Spirit dwells in it.

The people of God carry this creative presence of the Spirit with them on their pilgrim journey, much like when God had the Israelites make a sanctuary for him so that he could dwell among them on their journey from bondage to freedom, from slavery in Egypt to the promised land (Ex 25:8). Although worldwide synods are "privileged places in which the Church experiences the action of the Holy Spirit,"[8] the Spirit is always with the church in its many synodal processes from the smallest parish to the worldwide church, guiding it in its communal discernment as it seeks the path forward, and enabling it to "worship in spirit and truth" (Jn 4:24).

BAPTISMAL SPIRITUALITY

Although the baptismal foundation of a synodal church was explored in chapter 1, the present chapter discusses how a synodal spirituality is baptismal, rooted as it is in a baptismal ecclesiology. Martin Luther's admonition to "return to your baptism daily" is one profitably taken to heart by all Christians. Luther advised, "Therefore let all Christians regard their Baptism as the daily garment that they are to wear all the time. Every day they should be found in faith and with its fruits, suppressing the old creature and growing up in the new."[9] In baptism the people of God begin a journey of initiation. Although received in its entirety with the invocation of Father, Son, and Spirit with immersion or effusion, baptism is not a closed event at the moment of its celebration. Baptism initiates a Christian into a pilgrim church on the move because it elicits a lifelong response in faith and discipleship. It represents a journey of ever-deepening communion with God and fellowship with other Christians. In baptism we are made holy and yet can grow in holiness. As the *Instrumentum Laboris* for the Second Session of the Synod on Synodality observes, baptism is a gift that should be nourished "through the commitment to conversion, service to mission and participation in the life of the community."[10] This baptismal journey is dynamic and transformative, a far cry from a static and individualistic view of initiation as well as salvation.

Baptism really encompasses three interrelated processes: the baptismal rite itself consisting of the pouring of water in the name of Father, Son, and Spirit; an expanded rite of initiation in the Ordo of the Christian Initiation of Adults; and a baptismal pattern of living. These are related to one another as a threefold series of recapitulations. The briefer form becomes a shorthand for the next expanded rite of initiation, which in turn indicates what is lived in day-to-day Christian living in a Christian pattern of life.[11] Consequently, the renunciations of evil and the recitation of the creed in the baptismal rite summarize the work of conversion in the catechumenate within an expanded rite of initiation. The catechumenate, a time of conversion and Christian formation for Christian living, prepares a person for the ongoing life of Christian discipleship and missionary synodality. Formation based on the dynamism of Christian initiation aims to form witnesses, that is, "men and women capable of assuming the mission of the Church in co-responsibility and cooperation with the power of the Spirit (Acts 1:8)" by promoting "the personal experience of encounter with the Lord that entails a process of continuously converting our attitudes, relationships, mentality, and structures."[12] In this way, baptism becomes a pattern for all of life, another reason why a synodal spirituality is rooted in a baptismal spirituality.

Baptism sacramentally enacts the journey of a synodal church and all of Christian life in union with Christ back to the Father within the process of a reconciliation of all in Christ. Baptism calls us to walk daily in the newness of Christian life by practicing a Christian ethic that connects the new creature we have become in Christ with the goal of humanity as revealed in Christ. Living out baptismal identity leads to sacrificial service. Thus, the faith with which we receive in baptism finds expression in love, which in turn impels us to mission. As Christ was sent on mission, so we are sent to build up the city of God on earth. As Christ returns to his Father after completing his task, so too, do we look forward to a union with the Father when we will see him face to face. Baptism is essentially eschatologically oriented, as a synodal, pilgrim church is eschatologically oriented because the newness effected in baptism, although complete insofar as we are justified in baptism, remains incomplete or at risk insofar as the new creation is not fully realized in historical time. A pilgrim church instantiates in history and cultures what baptism signifies in sacramental sign. Thus, aspects of the "already" and the "not yet" are intrinsic to baptism as they are to all sacraments and a church on pilgrimage.

All of Christian life is properly baptismal because Christians assume an identity that reorients the whole of life. Christians put on Christ when plunged into his death and resurrection in the baptismal waters and enter the church by way of the baptismal font. The whole of Christian life is paschal both in its structure and in its spirituality identified as a dying to sin, selfishness, and inordinate attachments and a rising to new life in Christ in the freedom of the Spirit. As such, a baptismal spirituality is cruciform. Baptism, which incorporates us into the once-for-all death of Christ, calls us to a daily dying to sin and rising to new life and is a continuing call to repentance, faith, and obedience to Christ. Having become a Christian when baptized, Christians grow into their Christian identity, deepening it over a lifetime. This means that the new creation effected in the modality of sacramental sign, although real and efficacious in terms of grace, is lived out and comes to full embodiment in the everydayness of human interactions in a process involving duration and development within historical time. We die to sin and rise in the grace of God over a lifetime. Baptism is truly foundational in that baptism contains all of Christian life in a nutshell.

EUCHARISTIC SPIRITUALITY

A synodal spirituality is Eucharistic. In Catholic sacramental theology, *viaticum*, the name given to holy communion given to a dying person, literally means "provision for a journey." *Viaticum* accompanies the dying person on their journey to God from this life to the next. However, in a broader sense, all Eucharistic sharing is *viaticum*, food for the journey.[13] Just as the Israelites were fed manna in the desert, so, too, the pilgrim people of God are fed the Eucharist to sustain them on this journey through life.

The liturgical rite of the Eucharist calls us to justice. Since the bread offered at the Eucharist is "the fruit of the earth and work of human hands," it calls us to the just distribution of resources, to feeding the hungry, and to care of the land. It makes us mindful of those who grow our food and their living conditions, perhaps as migrant workers. It invites us to an examination of conscience by asking who is included at the table? Who is excluded from it? This not only the table of the Eucharist, but also the table of opportunity in terms of education, housing, health services and income. We are called to see and repent of our discrimination and prejudices. Finally, it calls us to serve one another by preparing the feast and being true companions on the way, literally those who break bread together.

The church is called to practice an inclusive hospitality reflective of Jesus's table fellowship with tax collectors and sinners. In the past, our Eucharistic ecclesiology has functioned to delineate boundaries between church members and nonmembers, between those Catholics in a "state of grace" admitted to communion and those whose moral lives has placed them in a state of alienation from the community. This has included the divorced and remarried Catholics and others in irregular unions excluded from the Eucharist as well as the LGBTQ+ community. Traditionally, the church has considered a sacrament to be both a sign of grace and a means of grace, but the emphasis has been placed more heavily on the sign than on the means. Can we find a way for our ecclesial table fellowship to mirror more closely that table fellowship with sinners practiced by Jesus in the Gospel? It takes a lot of catechesis to explain the ecclesial symbolism of the Eucharist and why those outside of communion with the church are also outside of Eucharistic communion. On the other hand, we have succeeded so well with our teaching that people are fed with the body of Christ in the Eucharist, that enforced exclusion from the Eucharist elicits the primordial emotions associated with starvation and the profound, wrenching embarrassment of exclusion. Some consider that our experience of access to the table has become casual and is taken for granted. However, the tears and pain of those excluded because they belong to another Christian church or are in an irregular marriage is evidence to the contrary. As a church we are challenged to minister to these fellow Christians with compassion and to discover new paths to reconciliation.

The varied contrasting responses to the infamous footnote 351 in Pope Francis's *Amoris Laetitia* reveals the ecclesial divide on this issue.[14] He had suggested that "because of forms of conditioning and mitigating factors, it is possible that in an objective situation of sin—which may not be subjectively culpable, or fully such—a person can be living in God's grace, can love and can also grow in the life of grace and charity, while receiving the Church's help to this end." The footnote states that "in certain cases, this can include the help of the sacraments" and, citing *Evangelii Gaudium*, that the Eucharist "is not a prize for the perfect, but a powerful medicine and nourishment for the weak." A return to a theology of the Eucharist as *viaticum* for pilgrims on the way, a holy people yet also a sinful people, and a church also holy, yet also always in need of purification (*LG* 8), in service of a Christ, who was "made to be sin who knew no sin, so that in him we might become the righteousness of God" (2 Cor 5:21), evokes Jesus's table fellowship with sinners (Mt 9:10–17; Mk 2:15–22; Lk 5:29–39). When the Pharisees rebuked Jesus for this, he replied, "Those who are well have no need of a physician, but those who are sick: I have come to call not the righteous but sinners" (Mk 2:17). The people of God on pilgrimage are invited to this fellowship.

FREEDOM, RECONCILIATION, AND MERCY

The journey to God is both a journey of growth in freedom and a journey undertaken in freedom. The journey of the Israelites in the desert was a journey from slavery toward freedom: "And I will walk among you, and will be your God, and you will be my people; I, the Lord, am your God who brought you out of the land of Egypt to be their slaves no more; I have broken the bars of your yoke and made you walk erect" (Lv 26:12–13). From slavery, they were formed into a people identified by the God they worshipped. The journey strengthened them in this identity even as their faith was tested, and they murmured against the hardships they suffered. They received the law of the Lord, were nourished by manna, and learned to follow the Lord, whether in a pillar of cloud by day or by a pillar of fire by night (Ex 11:21).

In common parlance, freedom is thought to be the ability to do whatever one wants. In Ignatian spirituality, however, freedom is more akin to indifference understood as "an attitude of equipoise."[15] For Ignatius, "indifference" does not mean "not caring," but freedom from our non-freedoms. Negatively, freedom is the absence of disordered affections and attachments that prevent a person from pursuing praise, love, and service of God and love of neighbor—in other words, "a positive desire for God and his will."[16] Positively, indifference "is an affective space within which the movements of the Spirit can be sensed and things seen in relation to the signs of God's will, an affective silence making possible an unconditional listening."[17] Indifference is being unconstrained by external and internal obstacles to genuine choosing. Indifference is something one grows into as one progresses in the spiritual life and responds to a deep desire to do whatever is necessary to praise, love, and serve God, to follow Christ, and to live the Gospel. A spirituality of Ignatian indifference is important for synodality as a precondition for deep listening and discernment.

Likewise, the notion of the "will of God" needs clarification. The "will of God" is not some detailed blueprint for our life that we must decipher, but human flourishing in relation to God and neighbor—essentially love, although that word has too often become hackneyed in popular culture. Desire to do the will of God enflames the affectivity that is the work of the Spirit directing and pointing the way to God. While the theological language of "will of God" and "indifference" sometimes sounds sterile and technical, images from poetry and scripture help to put flesh on abstract bones and refresh hackneyed expressions.

Jesus's mission was one of freedom. After his temptation in the desert, Jesus returned to Galilee to Nazareth, his hometown, and read from the prophet Isaiah: "The Spirit of the Lord is upon me, because he has anointed me, to bring good news to the poor. He has sent me to proclaim release to the captives and recovery of sight to the blind, to let the oppressed go free, to proclaim the year of the lord's favor" (Lk 4:18–18). His entire public ministry then put this into action. Jesus freed the blind by giving back sight, the paralytic by giving back motion, the poor by giving them hope, from illness by restoring health, from sin by forgiving. Then, in John's account of the Resurrection and the gift of the Spirit, Jesus appeared to the disciples through locked doors, frees them from fear, saying "Peace be with you." He shows them his wounds in his hands and his side, not only proving that yes, this is indeed Jesus who was crucified, but also *who* Jesus is, the God of mercy who frees from sin through his wounds, passion, and death, the God who elicits doubting Thomas's profession of faith, "My Lord and my God" (Jn 20:28). In this Gospel scene, freedom and mercy burst through the locked doors of fear as Christ reveals divine mercy.

In this same scripture passage Jesus breathes on the disciples and says, "Receive the Holy Spirit." In Acts, the Spirit take the form of tongues of fire, but here, the Spirit is the breath of Christ, the same breath he surrendered to the Father at his moment of death saying, "Father, into your hands I commend my Spirit" (Lk 23:46) when he breathed his last. The Spirit as breath represents freedom for the Spirit blows where it will (Jn 3:8). Disciples on pilgrimage are called to a spirituality of freedom in the Spirit, Christ's Spirit, to be sent into the world as he was sent, called in freedom to do the works of the Spirit in freeing others.

Such freedom might also be compared to the freedom of dance, the fluidity of motion free from bodily tension, or to vocal freedom where free, soaring sound emerges from an open throat free of all constriction. Freedom is an image of Lazarus being raised from the dead, for Jesus's instructions were, "Unbind him, and let him go" (Jn 11:44). When Jesus himself rose from the dead he left his binding burial cloths behind (Jn 20:6–70). These images help us to imagine embodied freedom.

With the gift of the Spirit, Christ commissions his disciples to continue his mission of freedom: "As the Father has sent me, so I send you" (Jn

20:21). This mission is none other than a mission of reconciliation: "Receive the Holy Spirit. If you forgive the sins of any, they are forgiven them; if you retain the sins of any, they are retained" (Jn 20:22–23). While we tend to associate this ministry with the ordained in the Sacrament of Reconciliation or to the authority of the church, this post-resurrection mission to free people through forgiveness is given to the entire people of God. In the new creation, God "who reconciled us to himself through Christ, and has given to us the ministry of reconciliation; that is, in Christ God was reconciling the world to himself, not counting their trespasses against them, and entrusting the message of reconciliation to us" (2 Cor 5:18–18). As the Gospel repeatedly reiterates, forgiveness is the way of the Christian: "Forgive and you will be forgiven" (Lk 6:37); "forgive us our sins for we ourselves forgive everyone indebted to us" (Lk 11:4); and "If another disciple sins, you must rebuke the offender, and if there is repentance, you must forgive. And if the same person sins against you seven times a day and turns back to you seven times and says, 'I repent,' you must forgive" (Lk 17:3–4). The pilgrim's way is one of reconciliation.

Sin is unfreedom and the epitome of all that binds. The sins we retain are when we refuse to free, to unbind, and to forgive. Jesus entered a locked room showing the wounds of his mercy. He gives us the Spirit, the empowerment, and love to continue this work. He then sends us out to live in the freedom of the Spirit and to free others from all that bind, to extend mercy. Yet, it is important to note that mercy is broader than forgiveness of sins and what might be considered sin is broader than discrete transgressions; that is, specific acts of sin or culpable non-actions or omissions.

First and foremost, sin is a breach of a relationship with God. This breach may occur through sinful actions, but a contemporary understanding of sin has broadened under the influence of secularization to account for a more dynamic view of sin in relation to the history of salvation and the solidarity of salvation.[18] For Bernard Häring, from this broader perspective sin is "total alienation from God, from faith, from adoration, from knowledge of God, and from our fellow men [sic]."[19] He asserts that "atheism and secularism are the most complete embodiments of sinfulness and manifest the deepest roots of sin insofar as the loss of the sense of sin and manifold alienations" result from the refusal "to know and adore God."[20] Here, knowledge is not just knowledge *about* God, but rather an experiential knowledge *of* God; alienation is not only a condition of being *against* God, but the *absence* of a relationship with God. Simply put, life is *experienced* as being functionally Godless.[21] This alienation may itself result in no small part from a kind of truncated and static moral theology that divorces moral action from its roots in the moral agency of an individual in responsive and responsible relationship with God and her fellow human beings.

Moral responsiveness, however, must go beyond external conformity to law. This moves a theology of sin from a moral level to a religious level, to a morality and spirituality of conversion and renewal.[22] This is where forgiveness can be distinguished—at least in part—from mercy, although the two are closely interrelated. For example, the synodal document "Towards a Spirituality for Synodality" states, "The Father offers us His forgiveness, not as a sole act that touches only our past; on the contrary, He bathes our entire life in the waters of mercy. Therefore, not only are we always forgiven (and forgivable) by God but, somehow, we are constantly offered the opportunity to live through mercy and to share it with others."[23] Forgiveness occurs at specific points in time, but mercy is a permanent, ongoing state. Mercy includes forgiveness but also exceeds it. Where forgiveness has acts, dispositions, omissions, and transgressions as its object, mercy is directed to the totality of an individual in his or her condition of pitiable need, poverty, total dependence, and sinfulness.

Mercy has been a major theme of the twenty-first century and figures prominently in the last three pontificates. Pope John Paul II established Divine Mercy Sunday in 2000 and his second encyclical was *Dives in Misericordia* (1980). He stated that the boundary that has been set for evil "is ultimately divine mercy."[24] Pope Benedict XVI continued the theme in *Deus Caritas Est* (2005) and *Caritas in Veritate* (2009). Arguably, it is the central theme in the pontificate of Francis in *Evangelii Gaudium* (2013), *Fratelli Tutti* (2020), and in his personal reflections in *The Church of Mercy*.[25] An additional influence is Walter Kasper's book, *Mercy: The Essence of the Gospel and the Key to Christian Life*, which appeared in German in 2012, one year before the election of Pope Francis, and in English in 2014.[26]

Pope Francis signals the centrality of mercy by his choice of his episcopal moto, *Miserando atque eligendo,* a phrase from a homily by the Venerable Saint Bede describing Jesus's call of Saint Matthew that occurs in the church's daily prayer readings for Saint Matthew's feast day, September 21. The whole Latin phrase and its translation are:

> "*Vidit ergo Jesus publicanum, et quia miserando atque eligendo vidit, ait illi, 'Sequere me'*" might be translated as "Jesus therefore sees the tax collector, and since he sees by having mercy (or by looking at him with the eyes of mercy) (or by "mercy-ing" him, as the Holy Father has translated it) (*miserando*) and (*atque*) by choosing (*eligendo*), he says to him, "Follow me."[27]

Here, Pope Francis turns "mercy" into a verb. More than the forgiveness of the tax collector's extortion and theft, sinful actions, Jesus looks on the condition of the whole person with pity and steadfast love, a quality of mercy. He chooses Matthew and bids him to follow him. In doing this, he calls him from one way of life to another, from his allegiance to money to allegiance to Jesus, from his despicable condition to full potential in fulfilling his purpose as a human being. This call to conversion addresses the whole person, not simply certain acts.

For Pope Francis, mercy is the content of the proclamation of the Gospel, the message that "Jesus Christ loves you; he gave his life to save you; and now is living at your side every day to enlighten, strengthen, and free you."[28] The Parable of the Good Samaritan represents this proclamation in action. Pope Francis calls it "pure Gospel" and devotes the entirety of chapter 2 of *Fratelli Tutti* to it.[29] In this parable, individuals and the entire church are called to minister to the wounds of the traveler lying on the side of the road. Yet, we as individuals and the entire church—as recent scandals have shown—are also that traveler on the road in need of healing. We are both in need of mercy and are called to extend mercy. Not only the ministers of the church, but all the pilgrim people of God must be agents of mercy, accompanying people and healing their wounds. To do this, however, they themselves need to "experience this healing power first-hand in their own wounds, as individual persons and as a body."[30] Only then, Francis adds, "will we lose the fear of letting ourselves be moved by the immensity of our brothers' and sisters' suffering."[31]

What, exactly, is this mercy, and what is its relationship to justice and forgiveness? To go to the Old Testament origins, important concepts include "heart," "*hānan*" and "*hesed*," and *rehem or rahāmīm*. *Hesed* means "unmerited loving kindness, friendliness, favor, and also divine grace and mercy."[32] *Hesed* is translated in the Septuagint as *eleos* (mercy), corresponding to *hānan* in the Hebrew bible, where it means to show favor to someone because of their possession of *hen*, the trait, quality, or disposition on the basis of which one is found pleasing.[33] The Septuagint translates *hen* as *charis* (grace as gift received).[34] *Hesed* is "a basic posture that incarnates itself in deeds of kindness and friendship," as "surpassing the purely obligatory and expected," as "surprising acts of kindness," and as "overwhelming, astonishing graciousness that is oblivious of itself and solely for the other."[35] "Heart" describes "the core of the human person, the seat of his or her feelings as well as the seat of his or her power of judgment."[36] In the Bible, God chooses people according to his heart (1 Sm 13:14; Jer 3:15; Acts 13:22). In Genesis 6:6, God regretted having made humankind on the earth on account of their evil, and "it grieved him to his heart." For the ancients, the intestines are the seat of feelings and express the mercy that comes from the heart.[37] *Hesed* is often used in conjunction with '*emet*, faithfulness. So, as Duffy explains, "*hesed* is one of the most important liturgical predicates of God when the Tanach celebrates God as a God of people: God is 'a merciful and gracious God, long-suffering and rich in *hesed* and '*emet* (Ex 34:6f.)."[38] He continues, "*rehem* refers to the maternal womb (Jer 20:17) and *rahāmīm*, its abstract plural, connotes passionate maternal love, hence mercy (e.g., Hos 11:8)."[39] Duffy summarizes all this word study in terms of Israel's experience of grace as God's dynamic love revealed in unexpected acts: "*Hānan* stresses God's gracious presence to and concern for people, and especially the divine solidarity with the weak and oppressed. *Hesed* emphasizes a love transcending duty, a love unmerited and overflowing in abundance."[40]

Ronald Witherup summarizes this broad and deep biblical vocabulary of mercy as including the concepts of "mercy, graciousness, kindness, pity, compassion, empathy, steadfast faithfulness, favor, and love."[41] Coming from the depths of one's being, it is the "ability to enter into another's suffering and pain and to offer saving, life-giving help."[42] For our purposes, what is significant is that all these Hebrew words in some way express God's passionate, maternal, faithful, kind, and gratuitous relationship to his people that does not at all evoke a tribunal of pardon in such a way that mercy is reduced to simply being equivalent to forgiveness. Mercy is much more than forgiveness, even though the two go together, and we are challenged as a church to liturgically celebrate a mercy that is oriented to a human condition that is not totally captured by transgressions or omissions, or even by attitudes and dispositions. We have a hard time naming sin, or at least getting to the root of whatever that human posture before God is that cries out for mercy.

Mercy is a countermeasure against any temptation to attitudes of superiority or contempt toward others or legal systems of retribution. Far from signaling a position of superiority of the person extending mercy to someone subordinate to them and thereby reinforcing hierarchical relationships at the expense of relationships of equality, the people of God stand in solidarity with one another as fellow travelers, also wounded and in need of mercy and the healing touch of others and Jesus Christ. We accompany one another, tending to one another's wounds and thereby continuing the ministry of Christ. As Cardinal Walter Kasper puts it, "the Christian form of mercy is ultimately Christian existence on behalf of others."[43]

If the risen Christ extends to us the mission of reconciliation and forgiveness of sin (Jn 20:21–23; 2 Cor 5:19), no less does he extend to us the mission of mercy, saying "Blessed are the merciful, for they will receive mercy" (Mt 5:7). This call to action evokes the mutual and reciprocal relationship of mercy: mercy given, and mercy received. Pope John Paul II underscores this reciprocity, saying, "An act of merciful love is only really such when we are deeply convinced at the moment that we perform it that we are at the same time receiving mercy from the people who are accepting it from us."[44] He calls it "the most perfect incarnation of 'equality' between people."[45] Although mercy is, in the words of Witherup, "the quintessential aspect of God,"[46] it is also the teaching of Jesus of Nazareth, and that same mercy is an essential characteristic of Christians, who are admonished, "Be merciful just as your Father is merciful" (Lk 6:36). This text became the source of the official motto, *Misericordes Sicut Pater* (Merciful Like the Father) of Francis's Bull of Indiction for the Extraordinary Jubilee of Mercy on December 8, 2015, entitled *Misericordiae Vultus*.[47]

Pope John Paul II established Divine Mercy Sunday on the second Sunday of the Easter season and penned an encyclical on mercy, *Dives in Misericordia* (1980), in which he identified mercy as belonging to the mission of the church that must bear witness to the mercy of God revealed in Christ, not only proclaiming it, but also making it incarnate in the lives of the faithful and in those of people of good will.[48] In addition to belonging to the mission of the church, mercy is also "a whole lifestyle and continuous characteristic of the Christian vocation."[49]

Emphasis on the mercy of God has social, political, and ethical implications for mutual relationships in a synodal church. The corporal and spiritual works of mercy by which we come to the aid of our neighbor are deeply embedded in the Catholic tradition. The corporal works of mercy are to feed the hungry, give drink to the thirsty, shelter the homeless, visit the sick and imprisoned, visit prisoners, bury the dead, and give alms to the poor.[50] The spiritual works of mercy are to counsel the doubtful, instruct the ignorant, admonish the sinner, comfort the sorrowful, forgive injuries, bear wrongs patiently, and pray for the living and the dead.[51] More than individual acts from person to person, these works of mercy are also the basis of corporate social initiatives undertaken by the church, other religious groups, or nonprofit organizations. One thinks of such groups as Catholic Charities, Caritas Internationalis, Catholic Relief Services, the St. Vincent de Paul Society, and Bread for the World, just to cite some examples.

Mercy goes even further than interpersonal charity and mutual relationships; it is also "the most perfect incarnation of justice," although it also tempers justice with love and forgiveness.[52] It corrects distorted forms of justice manifested in such axioms as "an eye for an eye and a tooth for a tooth" or the so-called justice that aims to annihilate the enemy in exchange for wrongdoing. It does not seek revenge, which never guarantees peace for the victim. Peace and freedom are often restored only when a person can work through the pain and trauma to the point of being able to forgive the evil that has been done. This does not erase emotional scars or deep-seated hurt, but only at the point of forgiveness—not easy and never automatic—does the perpetrator of evil cease to have power over a victim.

Justice and mercy are correlative terms, the two often occurring together in scriptures. Thus, in Zechariah 7:9, the Lord says, "Administer true justice; show mercy and compassion to one another." In Micah 6:8, the Lord requires that one "do justice, love mercy (sometimes translated as 'kindness'), and walk humbly with your God." The Psalmist says, "Steadfast love and faithfulness will meet; righteousness and peace will kiss each other" (Ps 85:10). Mercy purifies justice, and justice ensures that mercy is not "cheap grace."[53] After all, sin and evil have social and interpersonal consequences in spite of mercy.

In sum, mercy is an attribute of a synodal church because as a social reality, it is always relational, with both personal and communal dimensions. Mercy summarizes the trajectory that Pope John XXIII set for the church in his opening address for the Second Vatican Council: "Nowadays, the Spouse of Christ prefers to make use of the medicine of mercy rather than that of severity. She considers that she meets needs of the present day by demonstrating the validity of her teaching rather than by condemnations."[54] The pope then comments that people have learned by experience that the imposition of force, the power of weapons, and political domination have not resolved the most serious questions. Consequently, he says that the Catholic Church "desires to show herself to be the loving mother of all, benign, patient, full of mercy and goodness toward the brethren who are separated from her."[55] In other words, mercy is what animates the pastoral intent of the council. The Second Vatican Council differed from previous councils in that it neither condemned theological positions as did the Council of Trent, nor did it issue definitive statements such as the teaching on papal infallibility at Vatican I. The fundamental aim of the council was "to make more room for charity . . . with clarity of thought and greatness of heart."[56] The pastoral orientation of the council meant that every aspect of the church's life was subordinated "to the demanding image of Christ as the good Shepherd."[57] John XXIII was looking for a "new Pentecost" so that the church's faith would come alive in a renewed spiritual awakening.[58]

This same spirit imbued Francis fifty-four years later, as expressed in his Apostolic Exhortation *Evangelii Gaudium* (2013), which essentially outlines the program of his pontificate. There he invites all Christians "to a renewed personal encounter with Jesus Christ" which liberates and infuses joy for those who seek Christ's mercy, enabling them "to embark upon a new chapter of evangelization marked by this joy, while pointing out new paths for the Church's journey in years to come" (*EG* 1, 3).

ECCLESIAL HUMILITY

Finally, a spirituality for a synodal, pilgrim church is incomplete without the virtue of ecclesial humility. Ecclesial humility is the virtue by which the church acknowledges its dependence on God and becomes other-centered rather than self-centered. Paul Lakeland calls it "a defining virtue of holiness" grounded in a sense of God's holiness.[59] With the virtue of humility, the church acknowledges not only its dependence on God, but also its limitations—limitations of knowledge, understanding, judgment, virtue, fidelity, and compassion. Ecclesial humility, the virtue of being close to the earth and in touch with the realities of life, supplies the antidote to ecclesial arrogance and triumphalism. Assurance that the charism of the indefectibility of the church preserves it in the truth necessary for salvation does not mean that the church possesses all truth, is correct in all its judgments, or always acts justly and charitably.

With this virtue, the church assumes a posture of reception and gratitude. Its humility derives from its gratitude for having received its whole life and mission from the Father, through Christ, in the power of the Spirit. For example, in humility, the magisterium recognizes that it is "not superior to the word of God, but is rather its servant" (*DV* 10). In humility, the church speaks the truth as it knows it, admitting that it does not have answers when as a pilgrim church it is still moving toward "the plenitude of divine truth until eventually the words of God are fulfilled in it" (*DV* 8). Questioning and probing characterize a pilgrim church that grows in its understanding of divine revelation, as *Gaudium et Spes*, the Pastoral Constitution of the Church in the Modern World, confirms (*GS* 21). Consequently, the church's pastors cannot be expected to have answers to all the complex questions that arise.

Ecclesial humility imitates the church's founder, Jesus Christ, who was humble and oriented to his Father. *Lumen Gentium* explains, "Henceforward the church, equipped with the gifts of its founder and faithfully observing his charity, humility and self-denial, receives the mission of proclaiming and establishing among all peoples the kingdom of Christ and of God, and is, on earth, the seed and the beginning of that kingdom" (*LG* 5). This text continues, "While it slowly grows to maturity, the church longs for the completed kingdom and, with all its strength, hopes and desires to be united in glory with its king" (*LG* 5). Here, in the opening paragraphs of *Lumen Gentium*, we have the characteristics of the pilgrim church in a nutshell: humility, the way of penance, the historicity of slow growth to maturity, and the destination of the journey in God.

In his opening remarks for the Synod on the Family, Pope Francis reminded the delegates that "the Synod will be a space for the action of the Holy Spirit only if we participants put on *apostolic courage, evangelical humility* and *trusting prayer*."[60] By evangelical humility, he means the attitude that enables one to overcome one's prejudices and attachments to the way things have always been done so that one may truly listen to another and be open to the presence of the Spirit in oneself and in another. Ecclesial humility does not rush to rash judgment or lord it over someone else with a false sense of superiority, but in a spirit of mercy, helps people, whatever their condition, to take the next step toward God. Ecclesial humility is not only a prerequisite for a synod but is an ongoing virtue indispensable for the discernment and deep listening needed for the church to be able to proclaim Christ's saving message of mercy within the pluralism inherent in particular times and places.

Humility both acknowledges the historically and culturally conditioned situation of the church requiring adaptation and respects that as a spiritual community and the mystical body of Christ, the church is also a mystery.[61] The historical conditioning of the church neither negates the mystery inherent to the church as described in the first chapter of *Lumen Gentium*, nor does it erase the continuity of its teaching and being, but rather it respects this mystery with the recognition that the church far exceeds what we experience and know of it at any step in its journey.[62] Likewise, as Paul Lakeland observes, since grace is the work of the Holy Spirit, humility requires "the recognition that the grace of God is spread throughout the world; that it is not coextensive with the church; and, indeed, that there is a worldly grace that the church does not control or even know."[63] The virtue of ecclesial humility respects divine mystery, acknowledges the presence of grace beyond the visible boundaries of the church, and the freedom of the breath Spirit to blow where it will.

Finally, humility characterizes leadership and authority in the church. In imitation of Jesus who washed the feet of his disciples, the church, at its best, exercises an authority of service. As *Lumen Gentium* states, "Ministers, invested with a sacred power, are at the service of their brothers and sisters" (*LG* 18). As already mentioned in chapter 1, Pope Francis explains,

> those who exercise authority are called "minister," because, in the original meaning of the word, they are the least of all. It is in serving the people of God that each bishop becomes, for that portion of the flock entrusted to him, *vicarius Christi*, the vicar of that Jesus who at the Last Supper bent down to wash the feet of the Apostles (cf. Jn 12:1–15). And in a similar perspective, the Successor of Peter is nothing else if not the *servus servorum Dei*.[64]

Humility is neither self-abasement nor self-deprecation, but the ability to be other-centered. A humble church is centrifugal, oriented to mission, rather than centripetal, oriented to self-preservation. It embodies Paul's hymn to love in 2 Corinthians 13:4–7: patient; kind; not envious, boastful or arrogant; not insisting on its own way; not rejoicing in wrongdoing but in the truth; hoping all things; enduring all things.

In humility, the church must confess that it has not always acted humbly. Pope John Paul II did just that at one of the ceremonies for the Jubilee, on March 12, 2000, when he asked for forgiveness of sins committed by members of the church, especially for sins committed in the name of the church. These included the use of "non-evangelical methods" in service of the faith such as at the time of the Inquisition, sins that caused divisions among Christians, sins against the Jews, sins against respect for other cultures and religions, sins that wounded the dignity of women and children, that marginalized the poor and violated the unborn. A few days later, from March 21 to March 26, the pope completed a pilgrimage to the Holy Land where he placed a copy of the prayer for forgiveness for sins against the Jews into a crack in the Western Wall.

Yet, all too sadly, sins of arrogance, greed, sexual abuse of children, and careerism persist. Power is not always exercised evangelically. Pope Francis on multiple occasions decries as a scourge on the church a clericalism that abrogates all power and prestige to itself. Some prelates are found guilty of child abuse, others become schismatic, and some misuse their authority. The church struggles to know how to welcome and relate to whole categories of people such as the divorced and remarried, immigrants, young people, women, racial minorities, those with disabilities, those with various addictions, and LGBTQ+ persons. For example, in the continental listening sessions for the first session of the Synod on Synodality, this struggle was evident in such comments as,

> "we think we are welcoming, but we know that there are people who feel 'outside' the Church" (Session III Group 12). Another suggested that this is because "we get caught up in the minutiae of evaluating the worth of people on the margins" (Session VIII Group 14). "There is a need to differentiate between the importance of teaching and the need to welcome those into the Church, especially as it relates to our LGBTQ+ brothers and sisters" (Session II Group 4).[65]

These responses reflect the indisputable fact that some individuals feel excluded by the church, that judgment of moral actions and those on the margins sometimes translates into a judgment of human worth, and that church members struggle to navigate the tension between upholding official church teaching and being more inclusive by welcoming those who live and think differently. While affirming the doctrine that it has discerned by listening both to the word of God and to the witnesses to the faith throughout the tradition of the church, a humble church does not weaponize this doctrine against its perceived enemies, against those people who are unable in conscience to affirm it, or against the weak who may fall short of its demands.

The antidote to sins of pride, abuse of power, and clericalism lies in ecclesial and personal humility. Tensions between church teaching and inclusivity and welcoming may never go away, but are navigated through deep listening to the experiences of others and through ongoing discernment. Deep listening may lead to increased tolerance, tolerance to compassion, and compassion to love. A synodal, pilgrim church in a posture of humility becomes a safe place where people can ask "real questions without judgment or punishment" and where they are accompanied at whatever stage of the journey they may find themselves.[66] The adoption of a humble, listening posture may also enable new insights into the doctrines to emerge, which give shape to new manners of teaching them. Traveling with another becomes a way of life, not simply an event in the life of the church.

CONCLUSION

A spirituality for a synodal, pilgrim church is Gospel-centered and Gospel-oriented, breathes the life of the Spirit in freedom, follows a pattern of journeying to life from death in the cruciform pattern of Christ's paschal mystery, practices a table fellowship of accompanying sinners and working for justice, embodies and promotes mercy and reconciliation, and is humble. Essentially, it is a spiritual pilgrimage in the footsteps of Christ as he journeyed back to his Father, taking its themes, attitudes, and practices from his cue. This spirituality, historically grounded in the realities, contradictions, and ambiguities of contemporary culture, does much more than imitate Christ; it participates in his divine life through the power of the Spirit as the church continues his mission.

NOTES

1. Richard Lennan, *Tilling the Church* (Collegeville, MN: Liturgical Press, 2022), 104.
2. Ignatius of Loyola, *The Spiritual Exercises*, trans. and commentary by George E. Gnass, SJ (Chicago: Loyola University Press, 1992), The First Principle and Foundation, §23.
3. Brouillette, *The Pilgrim Paradigm*, 173.
4. Ibid.
5. *IL*, Second Session, §27.
6. Francis, "Introductory Remarks, Synod for the Family," October 5, 2015, in *Walking Together*, 27.
7. Francis, "A Journey under the Guidance of the Holy Spirit," Letter to the Pilgrim People of God in Germany, June 29, 2019, in *Walking Together*, 83–99, at 88.
8. Francis, "Introductory Remarks, Synod for the Family," 27.
9. Martin Luther, *Large Catechism*, Fourth Part, 84–86, in *The Book of Concord: The Confessions of the Evangelical Lutheran Church*, trans. and ed. Robert Kolb and

Timothy J. Wengert (Minneapolis: Fortress Press, 2000), 466–67. Some of this material on baptismal spirituality is from Susan K. Wood, "'Return to your Baptism Daily': Baptism and Christian Life," in *Luther Refracted: The Reformer's Ecumenical Legacy,* ed. Piotr J. Małysz and Derek R. Nelson (Minneapolis: Fortress, 2015), 193–214.

10. IL, Second Session, §24.

11. Susan K. Wood, *One Baptism: Ecumenical Dimensions of the Doctrine of Baptism* (Collegeville, MN: Liturgical Press, 2009), 92–93.

12. IL, Second Session, §55.

13. Pope Francis referred to the Eucharist in his conversation with Anke de Bernadinis, the Lutheran wife of a Roman Catholic, who expressed sorrow at "not being able to partake together in the Lord's Supper." He said he asked himself: "Is sharing the Lord's Supper the end of the journey or is it the viaticum for walking together?" Francis, Address of His Holiness Pope Francis, Visit to the Evangelical Lutheran Church of Rome, Christuskirche Parish, November 15, 2015, https://www.vatican.va/content/francesco/en/speeches/2015/november/documents/papa-francesco_20151115_chiesa-evangelica-luterana.html.

14. Francis, Apostolic Exhortation *Amoris Laetitia* (The Joy of Love: On Love in the Family), March 19, 2016, §305, footnote §351, https://www.vatican.va/content/francesco/en/apost_exhortations/documents/papa-francesco_esortazione-ap_20160319_amoris-laetitia.html, citing in part EG 44.

15. Michael Ivens, SJ, *Understanding the Spiritual Exercises* (Leominster, MA: Gracewing, 1998), 31.

16. Ibid.

17. Ibid.

18. Bernard Häring, CSsR, *Sin in the Secular Age* (New York: Doubleday, 1974).

19. Ibid., 38.

20. Ibid., 40.

21. Here we are far from the usual matter for sacramental confession, but it does raise the question to sacramental theology of how to sacramentally celebrate the reconciliation of this existential alienation.

22. Häring, *Sin in the Secular Age*, 23.

23. Commission on Spirituality Sub-Group, "Towards a Spirituality for Synodality," 15.

24. John Paul II, *Memory and Identity: Conversations at the Dawn of a Millennium* (New York: Rizzoli, 2005), 55.

25. Pope Francis, *The Church of Mercy* (Chicago: Loyola Press, 2014).

26. Walter Kasper, *Mercy: The Essence of the Gospel and the Key to Christian Life*, trans. William Madges (New York: Paulist Press, 2014).

27. Deacon Tom Bello, OFS, "Miserando atque Eligendo," Secular Franciscan Order—USA, April 10, 2020, https://www.secularfranciscansusa.org/2020/04/10/miserando-atque-eligendo/; Cited by Wood, "Francis's Church Reform Focused on the Proclamation of Mercy: The Ignatian Influence," 11.

28. EG, §164.

29. Francis, Encyclical Letter *Fratelli Tutti*, October 3, 2020, §§56–86, https://www.vatican.va/content/francesco/en/encyclicals/documents/papa-francesco_20201003_enciclica-fratelli-tutti.html.

30. Francis, "Address of His Holiness Pope Francis to the 36th General Congregation of the Society of Jesus," General Curia of the Society of Jesus, October 24, 2016, https://www.vatican.va/content/francesco/en/speeches/2016/october/documents/papa-francesco_20161024_visita-compagnia-gesu.html.

31. Ibid.

32. Kasper, *Mercy*, 43.

33. Stephen J. Duffy, *The Dynamics of Grace: Perspectives in Theological Anthropology*, New Theology Studies 3 (Collegeville, MN: Liturgical Press, 1993), 19–20. See also Dominik Markl, "Divine Mercy in the Ancient Near East and in the Hebrew Bible," in *Raḥma: Muslim and Christian Studies in Mercy*, ed. Valentino Cottoni, Felix Körner, and Diego R. Sarrió Cucarella, Collection "Studi Arabo-Islamici del PISA!" vol. 22, 39–48. Rome: Pontificio Instituto di Studi Arabi e d'Islamistica, 2018.

34. Duffy, *Dynamics of Grace*, 20.

35. Ibid., 20–21.

36. Ibid.

37. Kasper, *Mercy*, 42.

38. Duffy, *Dynamics of Grace*, 21.

39. Ibid., 21–22.

40. Ibid., 23.

41. Ronald D. Witherup, PSS, *Mercy and the Bible: Why It Matters!* (New York: Paulist Press, 2018), 72.

42. Ibid., 92.

43. Kasper, *Mercy*, 150.

44. John Paul II, Encyclical, *Dives in Misericordia*, November 30, 1980, §14, https://www.vatican.va/content/john-paul-ii/en/encyclicals/documents/hf_jp-ii_enc_30111980_dives-in-misericordia.html.

45. John Paul II, *Dives in Misericordia*, §14.

46. Witherup, *Mercy and the Bible*, 72.

47. Francis, papal bull, *Misericordiae Vultus* (The Face of Mercy), April 11, 2015, https://www.vatican.va/content/francesco/en/bulls/documents/papa-francesco_bolla_20150411_misericordiae-vultus.html.

48. John Paul II, *Dives in Misericordia*, VII: The Mercy of God in the Mission of the Church.

49. John Paul II, *Dives in Misericordia*, §14.

50. *Catechism of the Catholic Church* (New York: Burns & Oates, 1999), §2447.

51. Ibid.

52. John Paul II, *Dives in Misericordia*, §14.

53. Dietrich Bonhoeffer, a German Protestant pastor who opposed national socialism, was executed in 1945 for his ties to the July 20, 1944, conspiracy to overthrow the Nazi regime. His famous quote is, "Cheap grace is grace without discipleship, grace without the cross, grace without Jesus Christ." Bonhoeffer, *The Cost of Discipleship* (New York: Macmillan, 1966).

54. John XXIII, *Gaudet Mater Ecclesia* (Mother Church Rejoices), October 11, 1962, published as "Pope John XXIII's Opening Speech to the Council," in *Documents of Vatican II*, ed. Walter M. Abbott (New York: America Press, 1966), 710–19, at 716.

55. Ibid.

56. John XXIII, in 1959, cited in Giuseppe Alberigo, *A Brief History of Vatican II* (Maryknoll, NY: Orbis, 2006), 9.

57. Ibid., 19.

58. John XXIII, Apostolic Constitution, *Humanae Salutatis*, December 25, 1961, published as "John XXIII Convokes the Council," in *Documents of Vatican II*, ed. Walter M. Abbott (New York: America Press, 1966), 703–9, at 709.

59. Paul Lakeland, "Reflections on the 'Grace of Self-Doubt,'" in *Ecclesiology and Exclusion: Boundaries of Being and Belonging in Postmodern Times*, ed. Dennis M. Doyle, Timothy J. Furry, and Pascal D. Bazzell (Maryknoll, NY: Orbis, 2012), 13–17, at 16.

60. Emphasis in the original. Francis, "Introductory Remarks, Synod for the Family," October 5, 2015, in *Walking Together*, 28.

61. See Gerard Mannion, *Ecclesiology and Postmodernity: Questions for the Church in our Time* (Collegeville, MN: Liturgical Press, 2007), 132–34; Lakeland, "Reflections on the 'Grace of Self-Doubt,'" 13–17; and "An Ecclesiology of Humility," in *A Council that Will Never End:* Lumen Gentium *and the Church Today* (Collegeville, MN: Liturgical Press, 2013).

62. See Susan K. Wood, "Continuity and Development in Roman Catholic Ecclesiology," *Ecclesiology* 7, no. 2 (May 2011): 147–72.

63. Lakeland, "Reflections on the 'Grace of Self-Doubt,'" 16–17.

64. Francis, Address at the Ceremony Commemorating the 50th Anniversary of the Institution of the Synod of Bishops.

65. "For a Synodal Church: Communion, Participation, and Mission," North American Final Document for the Continental Stage of the 2021–2024 Synod, 2023, §26. https://www.usccb.org/resources/North%20American%20Final%20Document%20-%20English.pdf.

66. Ibid., §32.

5

A Culture of Dialogue

The importance of faith-motivated dialogue is highlighted by the present culture, which has become increasingly uncivil. The current political scene is rife with toxic, demonizing, and demoralizing rhetoric. A synodal church with its centripetal rather than centrifugal focus cultivates a culture of respectful dialogue, especially with people whose views may differ markedly from our own. Such dialogue is the precondition for ecclesial discernment.

Dialogue—much more than a particular activity or way of proceeding within a synodal church—is the primary way of carrying out the mission of the church in the modern world. Pope Paul VI calls dialogue "a method of accomplishing the apostolic mission" in his 1964 encyclical letter, *Ecclesiam suam* [On the Church], much of which treats the nature and importance of dialogue.[1] Similarly, in a speech to Brazil's leaders several months after his election, Pope Francis commented,

> an element that I consider essential for facing the present moment is constructive dialogue. Between selfish indifference and violent protest there is always another possible option: that of dialogue. Dialogue between generations, dialogue within the people, because we are all that people, the capacity to give and receive while remaining open to the truth. A country grows when constructive dialogue occurs between its many rich cultural components: popular culture, university culture, youth culture, artistic culture, technological culture, economic culture, family culture and media culture: when they enter into dialogue. . . . When leaders in various fields ask me for advice, my response is always the same: dialogue, dialogue, dialogue.[2]

With these words, both Pope Paul VI, who established the Synod of Bishops as a permanent institution in 1965,[3] and Pope Francis, who convened the process for the Synod on Synodality (2021–2024), emphasize the importance of dialogue in the life of the church.

God's revelation gives us the paradigm and theological foundation for a culture of dialogue: God speaks; God's people are hearers of the Word; God's people respond. Dialogue has several dimensions: an individual's dialogue with God in prayer; dialogue with other people; dialogue within the church; and the dialogue of the church with the world, culture, and other faith traditions. Dialogue leads to both personal conversion and church reform.

As a description of communication within the church, the word "dialogue" is comparatively recent, not being found in preconciliar ecclesiology.[4] Dialogue arises within a context characterized by pluralism and the close proximity of those holding contrasting views, even within the same church or the same country. Gone are the days when homogeneity can be assumed.

THE NATURE OF DIALOGUE

Dialogue is essentially an encounter and conversation, a speaking and listening between partners. Each partner speaks from his or her context, from his or her perspective of viewing the world. Dialogic speech seeks to communicate that experience and perspective to the other and to receive that same message from the partner so as to be able to enter into as much as possible the experience of the other and so to see the other's perspective through their eyes. In speaking and in listening, we pay attention to what the Holy Spirit may be communicating through the other person. It is grounded in mutual respect for the dignity of the human person (*GS* 23, 40) and an attitude of listening to what the Holy Spirit says to us through another.[5]

Pope Francis's emphasis on dialogue within a synodal church implements a direction already indicated by the Second Vatican Council. For example, *Gaudium et Spes* promotes dialogue "with those who think or act differently from us in social, political, and even religious matters" (*GS* 28, 43), with unbelievers (*GS* 21), between cultures and groups of nations (*GS* 56), and in socioeconomic disputes (*GS* 68). *Ad Gentes*, the Decree on the Church's Missionary Activity, counsels that Christ's disciples learn "by sincere and patient dialogue" the treasures among the nations of the earth (*AG* 11).

Active Listening

Dialogue begins with deep, active listening to another. As Pope Paul VI said, before speaking, it is necessary to listen, not only to a person's voice, but to that person's heart.[6] This requires putting aside for the moment one's own agenda and fondly held positions to listen and explore what the other person has to say. This also requires listening to what lies beyond a person's words and listening to their emotions of joy, fear, or anxiety. It means listening to another's words as coming from their own context, not one's own. It means extending a hermeneutic of generosity by giving that person the benefit of the doubt and attributing the most positive meaning to what they are saying. It means not prejudging what that person is going to say before they even say it. We have to listen with our heart and not only our ears. It means listening with an attitude that we have something to learn from another. I should not be thinking about what I am going to say next, but seeking the truth in what another is saying.

Active listening begins with the attitude that we expect to hear the Spirit speaking to us through the other person. We may explore what the person is saying by means of follow-up questions or expressions of interest. We do not offer criticism or disagree with another if we think we have understood what the other person means. If we attempt to do this before trust is established, it will be difficult for the other person to be frank or sincere. We should allow ourselves to be affected by the other person, for dialogue engages the whole person. Active listening requires humility, openness, patience, and involvement.[7]

Pope Francis, in his homily at the occasion of the opening of the synodal path describes listening thus:

> Let us ask ourselves frankly during this synodal process: Are we good at listening? How good is the "hearing" of our heart? Do we allow people to express themselves to walk in faith even though they have had difficulties in life, and to be part of the life of the community without being hindered, rejected or judged? Participating in a Synod means placing ourselves on the same path as the Word made flesh. It means following in his footsteps, listening to his word along with the words of others. It means discovering with amazement that the Holy Spirit always surprises us, to suggest fresh paths and new ways of speaking. It is a slow and perhaps tiring exercise, this learning to listen to one another—bishops, priests, religious and laity, all the baptized—and to avoid artificial and shallow and pre-packaged responses. The Spirit asks us to listen to the questions, concerns and hopes of every Church, people and nation. And to listen to the world, to the challenges and changes that it sets before us. Let us not soundproof our hearts; let us not remain barricaded in our certainties. So often our certainties can make us closed. Let us listen to one another.[8]

Listening is not yet discerning, which will be discussed in the next chapter, but it is an essential step on the way to discernment. Hearing requires discernment to distinguish authoritative teaching from false teaching, but such discernment cannot bypass profound listening . . . listening to the word of God in scripture, to the word mediated through prophetic voices, to Jesus's authoritative teaching, to the word of God mediated through the wisdom of tradition, to the word of God in the cry of the poor and those who suffer, to the word of God in the signs of the times, and to the word of God embedded in the sanctuary of our hearts. It entails listening not only to our interlocuter, but also to the word of God, the tradition, the signs of the times, the church's teachers, the bishops, and all the people of God, including the poor and the marginalized. Listening may mean that we need to leave our own cultural and religious categories to enter those of another. This ability to listen is sorely needed in contemporary society and in church politics where in many ways we have lost the willingness to listen, a loss perhaps stemming from fear of those who are different from ourselves.

Intentional Speaking

In dialogue we also speak. We express ourselves, our experience, feelings, and thoughts. We speak the truth as we see it, not what we think others want to hear, not repeating someone else's truth that is also not our own.[9] As we speak, we need to be in touch with how we are responding interiorly to the other during the conversation, trying to free ourselves from selfish motivations in what we say. Such speaking requires both intellectual and emotional honesty, frankness, humility, and boldness. Pope Francis has said that synodality is exercised by "speaking honestly. . . with *parrhesia*" (candidly and without holding back) and listening with humility.[10] Other virtues of intentional speaking include, first of all, charity (1 Cor 13:1–2) followed by meekness, patience, generosity, and trust in one's own words and in welcoming the trust of the interlocutor, prudence in learning the sensitivities of the hearer.[11]

It entails sharing our personal perspective, values, and convictions informed by our experience, prayer, reading, and conversations with others. Finally, in dialogue we take responsibility for what we say and for what we are feeling, not blaming the other for what we feel.[12]

The first aim of dialogue is not to convince the partner of one's own deeply held convictions, but to understand another in a deep way. It is definitely not proselytism, which is any attempt to convert others to our own religious views, or the application of any form of religious or moral pressure, or any sort of manipulation. Dialogue respects freedom of conscience. Pope Francis has said, "It is not by proselytism that the

Church grows, but by 'attraction'" (*EG* 14). The Second Vatican Council's Decree on Religious Freedom (*Dignitatis Humanae*) states the principle of religious freedom thus:

> People grasp and acknowledge the precepts of the divine law by means of their own consciences, which they are bound to follow faithfully in all their activity, so as to come to God, their end. They must therefore not be forced to act against their conscience. Nor must they be prevented from acting according to it, especially in religious matters. The practice of religion of its very nature consists principally in internal acts that are voluntary and free, in which one relates oneself to God directly; and these can neither be commanded nor prevented by any merely human power. The social nature of human beings, however, requires that they should express these interior religious acts externally, share their religion with others, and witness to it communally. (*DH* 3)

Pope Francis reiterated his conviction concerning proselytism to the atheist Eugenio Scalfari, saying, "Our goal is not to proselytize but to listen to needs, desires and disappointments, despair, hope."[13]

Having established that dialogue is not proselytization, positive dialogue can be described as being above all a spiritual experience in understanding the other, a listening and a speaking to one another in love. Dialogue is more than an exchange of ideas. To borrow a phrase from Margaret O'Gara, herself inspired by John Paul II's *Ut unum sint*, dialogue is "a mutual gift exchange."[14] Dialogue is not only an exchange of ideas but also involves receiving the ethos of the other. Dialogue enables communion insofar as it involves accepting another person in his or her uniqueness and otherness, because dialogue is first and foremost a communication of persons before it is a communication of ideas. The aim is mutual sharing of ourselves, our values, our perspectives, and our faith before it is a sharing of ideas. The "gift" of dialogue is first of all ourselves. The ideas exchanged in dialogue are best grasped in the context of their lived embodiment in persons. Dialogue creates a relationship and establishes communion between persons.

Since we are a pilgrim community traveling along the way to the completed reign of God, we will of course be engaged in dialogue. "Pilgrimage" is an apt metaphor for dialogue, for dialogue entails a walking with the other. Dialogue represents a word on a common journey, neither the first word nor the last word. It marks a moment between the "already" of our past personal and communal histories and the "not yet" of our future. It is literally a word *in via*, a word "on the way" between pilgrims journeying alongside one another (*EG* 244).

Dialogue in a Pluralistic Culture

Dialogue is necessary because of the immense pluralism that exists both within the church and in the world. However homogenous the church may have seemed to have been from the Council of Trent to the Second Vatican Council due to such factors as the hegemony of a neo-scholasticism in theology, a centralized ecclesiastical government, and a Latin liturgy, those days are over, if they ever really existed. Too often, not only is the world to which some traditionalist would have us revert is not only irretrievably gone, but is also to some extent a naïve projection onto the past, rather than something that actually existed. As chapter 2 showed, plurality and reform has always been the order of the day, even when it has been resisted or eroded. Today, Catholic culture is characterized by a variety of theological methodologies and approaches to biblical criticism, renewed attention to enculturated local churches organized into regional episcopal conferences, and liturgies in the vernacular where it is not unusual for the Sunday liturgy to be celebrated in two or three dozen ethnic and linguistic communities. Pope Francis has encouraged the church to go to the peripheries.[15] This diversity, rather than being a challenge to the faith, represents an enrichment of the faith, the unity of which Pope Francis describes as a polyhedron rather than a sphere.[16] Yet, in spite of unity in creedal essentials of the faith and of communion in the same church, Catholics are not of the same mind and, at times, can be bitterly at odds on many matters of profound importance, whether these be questions of anthropology, education, foreign and domestic politics, or religious culture. Within such intellectual and cultural pluralism, dialogue is an imperative if we are to understand one another and be in community with one another rather than existing in our self-imposed silos of the like-minded. Yet, differences within a family can be much more acrimonious than differences among strangers. Dialogue in these circumstances can represent a real asceticism for our time and can serve as a crucible of purification.

The principle for such dialogue in a pluralistic context is given in *Gaudium et Spes*, the Pastoral Constitution of the Church in the Modern World:

> In virtue of its mission to spread the light of the gospel's message over the entire globe, and to bring all people of whatever nature, race or culture together into the one Spirit, the church comes to be a sign of that kinship which makes genuine dialogue possible and vigorous.
>
> This requires us first of all to promote mutual esteem, respect and harmony, with the recognition of all legitimate diversity, in the church itself, in order to establish ever more fruitful exchanges among all who make up the one people of God, both pastors and the rest of the faithful. For what unites the faithful is stronger than what divides them: there should be unity in essentials, freedom in doubtful matters, and charity in everything. (GS 92)

Here dialogue is directed toward mission. Interestingly, the goal is not to bring all people together into the one church, but to bring them together in the one Spirit, the church being a sign of that kinship. The principle of "unity in essentials, freedom in doubtful matters, and charity in everything" is reiterated in the *Unitatis Redintegratio,* the Decree on Ecumenism (*UR* 4), as a principle guiding ecumenical dialogue.

The question arises, however, of how one can possibly enter into dialogue when our minds are already made up or when the subject of dialogue is a teaching revealed by God and held firmly with a commitment of faith. Is it possible to have an open dialogue in this instance that is more than an exchange of opinions or personal views?[17] Does not dialogue presume that we are prepared to change our mind and alter our personal position? Is dialogue in this situation simply wanting to get along well with someone despite a difference of opinion or competing universal world views? While certain matters are definitive and irreversible, this does not mean that their expression cannot be refined through the improved understanding gained through dialogue. Even in situations where compromise or change is not possible and where essential dogmas of the faith are at stake, dialogue can result in the mutual and loving acceptance of another person, even when a unity of belief cannot be achieved. Much dialogue does not even concern such matters. Dialogue should aim at attempting to understand the attitudes, convictions, and orientation of those who differ from us. In doing this, dialogue creates relationships. It goes without saying that dialogue cannot be coercive but must be conducted in mutual freedom.

As we have noted, dialogue is not proselytism, that is, converting others to our own religious views. Nor is a synodal process, within which dialogue occurs, an instance of converting others to our own views. We share our experiences, beliefs, and values and deeply hear the experiences, beliefs, and values of our dialogue partners. In a group, consensus either emerges or we rest with our differences, but in communication with those who differ from us. Consensus is never coerced. Francis says that through mutual listening, "both parts can be purified and enriched" and express love for truth. Far from being a form of syncretism, true openness requires that the dialogue partners both remain steadfast in their convictions and clear in their identity while at the same time being open to understanding the convictions of the other party.

When we speak of a "willingness to change" as a result of dialogue, what is called for is the willingness to see the other in a different way and to change our patterns of thinking, speaking, and acting toward the other. Our understanding of another should resist the temptation to subsume the other into our own a priori theory of them, and perhaps be open to the development of a more inclusive narrative. Thus, we are called to explore theologies of healing and forgiveness in the search for openness to a transformed and reconciled relationship. This type of change results in a changed relationship to the other. There may also be intellectual positions that might end up changing through dialogue, whether concerning matters that are not definitive doctrine, or by improved understanding of what has been definitively taught, such that new pathways of development are possible. This is a change in how and what we think.

Dialogue with God

In 1964, Pope Paul VI identifed revelation as a dialogue in *Ecclesiam Suam* (§72), saying that revelation is the supernatural relationship which "God Himself, on His own initiative, has established with the human race," and that this relationship can be "represented as a dialogue in which the Word of God is expressed in the Incarnation and therefore in the Gospel."[18] The relationship between God and humans represents a conversation between them. In 1965, *Dei Verbum* set forth a similar dialogical dynamic with a treatment of the word of God within the economy of salvation.

This follows upon the very nature of God, for "In the beginning was the Word and the Word was with God, and the Word was God" (Jn 1:1). The first dialogue is actually within God in the intercommunion between the three persons. Jesus Christ, Word of God, sent into the world in history, is the self-communication of God to humans, who are constituted as hearers of the Word.[19] Humanity's first dialogue is with God, the dialogue in which God speaks his creative word and we receive our being. The dialogue continues within the dynamic of divine revelation and human response. The opening words of *Dei Verbum*, the Dogmatic Constitution on Divine Revelation, sets forth this dialogical character of the human person's relationship with God. God speaks, human beings hear and in turn speak, not only to God, but to others by proclaiming what they have heard:

> Hearing the word of God reverently and proclaiming it confidently, this holy synod makes its own the words of St. John: "We proclaim to you the eternal life which was with the Father and was made manifest to us—that which we have seen and heard we proclaim to you, so that you may have fellowship with us; and our fellowship is with the Father and with His Son Jesus Christ" (1 Jn 1:2–3). (*DV* 1)

The conciliar decrees of both the Council of Trent and the Second Vatican Council stress the interplay between hearing and speaking and mouth-to-mouth communication in the transmission of the divine word. For example, the Council of Trent states that "Our Lord proclaimed *with his own lips* the gospel, . . . then he bade it be *preached* to every creature . . . this truth and rule are contained in written books and in unwritten traditions which were received by the apostles *from the mouth* of Christ himself."[20] The Dogmatic Constitution on Divine Revelation (*Dei Verbum*) from Vatican II states its aim, following in the steps of Trent and Vatican I, "to set forth authentic teaching on God's revelation and *how it is communicated,* desiring that the whole world may *hear* the message of salvation, and thus grow *from hearing* to faith, from faith to hope, and from hope to love" (*DV* 1). *Dei Verbum* describes the pattern of revelation as God in his great love as *speaking* to humankind as friends (*DV* 2). Revelation unfolds through deeds and words. God has *spoken* through the *mouths* of the prophets (*DV* 14) and through his son, Jesus Christ, the Word made flesh (*DV* 4). Transmission of divine revelation repeats the orality already mentioned by the Council of Trent. Scripture is described as the *utterance* of God set down in writing (*DV* 9), which is disseminated by *preaching,* itself an oral act.

Clearly, the orality of transmission of revelation mirrors the human phenomenon of speaking and listening. This kind of communication requires a personal face-to-face encounter that establishes a relationship. It is not an exchange of information, but a communion of persons. The immediacy of the orality of revelation establishes the *kairos*, the right, critical, or opportune moment when God acts and invites human response.

In contemporary parlance the eyes are the windows of the soul, but in the ancient world the ear was the gateway to the soul. The great commandment in Deuteronomy begins, "Hear O Israel, The Lord is our God, the Lord alone! Therefore, you shall love the Lord, your God, with your whole heart, and with your whole being and with your whole strength." Jesus, the prophet, repeats this commandment and adds, "and your neighbor as yourself" (Mk 12: 29–31). A series of early Church Fathers held that Mary conceived Jesus through profound listening.[21] Jesus became flesh through Mary's hearing and assent to what she heard. Jesus, is, after all, the Word of God received by hearing.

The nature of revelation and the modality of the word invites a particular response because revelation is personal, relational, and dialogical.[22] The invited response corresponds to the modality in which the revelation is presented. When revelation is presented as a series of propositions to be assented to in faith or refuted, the response of faith is notional, a submission of intellect and will.[23] For example, chapter 1 of the Dogmatic Constitution on the Catholic Faith from Vatican I speaks of the revelation of the "eternal laws of his [God's] will."[24] Faith, from Trent to Vatican II, was primarily considered to be intellectual assent to these decrees.

Vatican II's Dogmatic Constitution on Divine Revelation (*Dei Verbum*), on the other hand, begins its account of divine revelation by identifying the fullness of revelation with Jesus Christ (*DV* 2). This corresponds to a personalistic notion of faith as a "total and free self commitment to God," although this constitution surprisingly treats the nature of the reception of revelation by faith in only one paragraph and largely repeats what has been said about faith at Vatican II, although placing the assent of faith by intellect and will in the broader context of total self-commitment (*DV* 5). It does not develop the personal aspect of faith in any detail, nor does it develop the dialogical character of faith. That awaited more adequate treatment in the Roman Catholic tradition in the *Catechism of the Catholic Church*, where faith is situated within the dialogical and personalistic context of invitation and response:

> By his Revelation, "the invisible God, from the fullness of his love, addresses men [sic] as his friends, and moves among them, in order to invite and receive them into his own company." The adequate response to this invitation is faith.[25]
>
> By faith, man [sic] completely submits his intellect and his will to God. With his whole being man [sic] gives his assent to God the revealer. Sacred Scripture calls this human response to God, the author of revelation, "the obedience of faith."[26]

The text then draws on a personal typology of faith, presenting Abraham and Mary as models of faith. It encompasses the complexity of faith as both personal adherence to God and assent to the truth of revelation in the statement, "Faith is first of all a personal adherence of man to God. At the same time, and inseparably, it is a *free assent to the whole truth that God has revealed*."[27] In this instance, the personal, relational, and dialogic character of both revelation and its response in faith are evident.

Revelation and the word of God are mediated. This is necessary according to the Thomistic dictum that "that which is received is received according to the mode of the receiver"[28] and the sacramental principle that God is present in and works through the fleshly, the finite, and the historical. In other words, whatever is communicated to another can only truly be received within the language, framework, and perspective of the hearer that mediates the message to that person. The locus of revelation is human experience. Dialogic speech engages the perspective of another and involves mutual sharing until the conversation partner is able to perceive the matter at hand through the perspective of the other. In this process, something of a fusion of perspectival horizons needs to occur. An example would be when an ecumenist is able to represent the position of a dialogue partner from another faith tradition, not only in terms that that person can recognize, but as faithfully as the partner would present his or her position. The world, including dialogic speech with another person, becomes a medium of God's self-communication, inviting discernment to seek God's presence there.

Dialogue within the Church

The role of the entire community in the preservation and active realization of the word of God represents a development in church teaching since the encyclical of Pius XII, *Humani Generis*. As Joseph Ratzinger points out, *Humani Generis* had stated in an antithetical way that the divine savior's word was entrusted "neither to the individual believers, nor to the theologians as such for its authentic explanation, but solely to the teaching office."[29] In contrast, *Dei Verbum* teaches that "in maintaining, practicing and professing the faith that has been handed on there is a unique interplay between the bishops and the faithful" (*DV* 10).

Dialogue within the church is theologically grounded in the teaching concerning the *sensus fidei* (sense of the faith), "the spiritual instinct that enables the believer to judge spontaneously whether a particular teaching or practice is or is not in conformity with the Gospel and with apostolic faith."[30] It is also grounded in the fact that all the faithful are active, participatory subjects in the church, as was developed in the first chapter. As such, they play "an active role in the development of Christian belief," that is, in the development of doctrine.[31] Their contribution to the *consensus fidelium* (consensus of the faithful) has, at times, helped to legitimize the definition of doctrine, although typically the sense of the faith by the faithful is more inchoate, instinctual, lived, or unthematic than expressed with theological precision.[32]

An intrinsic component of doctrinal teaching authority lies in the corporate and individual reception of magisterial teaching. The instinct of the faith, the *sensus fidei,* contributes to the reception of authentic teaching by the community based on the infallibility of the whole community in its supernatural discernment in matters of faith due to its anointing by the Holy Spirit (*LG* 12), an attribute known as the *sensus fidelium*.[33] Reception is here defined as "the process by which some teaching, ritual, discipline or law is assimilated into the life of the Church."[34] The emphasis is on a lived integration of teaching, not merely a notional agreement. Reception occurs when "the people of God adheres unwaveringly to the faith given once and for all to the saints, penetrates it more deeply with right thinking, and applies it more fully in its life" (*LG* 12), reinforcing the notion that reception occurs when teaching passes into the life of the church. Here the issue is not primarily with the juridical validity or even veracity of a teaching, but whether the teaching is efficacious, that is, whether it has a transformative power within a faith community.[35]

The text in *Lumen Genitum* juxtaposes this assertion about the role of the community with a statement about the role of the magistrium with this statement: "It [discernment in matters of faith] is exercised under the guidance of the sacred teaching authority, in faithful and respectful obedience to which the people of God accepts that which is not just the word of human beings but truly the word of God" (*LG* 12). In other words, the community has a kind of authority to recognize authentic teaching in its *sensus fidelium*, but this is exercised under the guidance of the magisterium to which the people of God are obedient. This might be seen as a dialectical tension, except that the magisterium is not separate from the people of God or over the people of God, but is itself part of the people of God, so the relationship is more complicated than simply two opposing authorities.

This type of juxtaposition is typical of a number of passages in the documents of Vatican II where two assertions tending in contrary directions are placed side by side in a sort of balance, but without any attempt at reconciliation.[36] Other examples include statements about the primacy and infallibility of the pope juxtaposed with statements about the collegiality of the bishops and the responsibility of all believers, or statements about the universal church juxtaposed with statements about the local churches. While Hermann Pottmeyer suggests that the juxtaposition of different theological positions within the final texts calls for a new synthesis by theologians after the council,[37] it may be helpful to consider the juxtaposition as a dialectic that needs to be retained in a certain amount of tension rather than be superceded by a new synthesis that obliterates the tension.[38] In such a view, the inerrancy of the whole people of God stands in dialectical tension with the authority of the magisterium. Both stand as true authorities, although with different modalities of expression. The magisterium is able to bring the faith to an expressed articulation that the entire people of God cannot. On the other hand, only the entire people of God can incorporate teaching and belief into its way of life that the magisterium cannot in and by itself. Authentic teaching requires both to be effective.

Dialogue within an Ecclesiology of Communion

Dialogue within the church is situated within an ecclesiology of communion. The 1985 Synod of Bishops identified "communion" as the dominant theme in the Second Vatican Council. Within a communion ecclesiology, the *communio fidelium* (communion of believers) is situated within the *communio ecclesiarum* (communion of churches). In the first thousand years, when the church was considered a communion of churches, the relationship among the churches was one of mutuality, shared communication, and mutual reception, which created a climate in which consensus could arise. In the second millennium up to Vatican II, with the growing centralization of the church that created a system of jurisdictional superiority and subordination, obedience constituted reception of church teaching and was the means of achieving unanimity. Within a renewed theology of a communion of churches, however, reception or consent constitutes a consensus.[39] As has been shown, the whole church, inclusive of the laity, is enlivened by the Spirit, is an active subject, and has the faculty of discernment, by which it can arrive at a consensus. Yves Congar, while noting that reception by the faithful "creates neither legitimacy nor a legal force of obligation . . . in the soundest Christian tradition, those *ministers exercising authority never act alone.*"[40] While reception does not confer legitimacy or validity on a conciliar decision and an authentic magisterial degree, it does attest to the presence of the Spirit working within the church and that the decision is good for the church.

Dialogue within a model of church as communion requires a community that is small enough to accommodate face-to-face communication.[41] Hermann J. Pottmeyer gives the following characteristics of this model of church, which applies to a synodal church:

- An organic connection between the universal Church and the local churches
- The cooperation between ordained office holders and lay people
- The theological necessity of both primacy and collegiality
- Unity within plurality[42]

Dialogue characterizes a synodal church in contrast to the emphasis on "jurisdiction" and "obedience" that predominated in a preconciliar ecclesiology characterized by Pottmeyer as:

- The priority of the universal church over the local church (universalist ecclesiology)
- The priority of the ordained office holder over the congregation and the charisms (clericalism)
- The priority of the monarchical over the collegial structure of office (centralism)
- The priority of unity over plurality (uniformity)
- One-way communication "from above to below" (superiority and subordinationism)[43]

Pottmeyer's description of a dialogical church in his 1994 book presages the synodal model proposed by Pope Francis where dialogue serves a synodal way of being church, characterized as a people on a journey, a pilgrim church which is missionary by her very nature.[44] Structural reform includes strengthening structures of collegiality, reforming the Curia, increasing the diversity of voices heard in the church, implementing structures of consultation such as synods on all levels of church life, and practicing subsidiarity by supporting initiatives of local churches.

DIALOGUE AND SYNODALITY

In a 2015 speech marking the fiftieth anniversary of the Synod of Bishops, Pope Francis said, "A synodal church is a listening church, knowing that listening 'is more than feeling.' It is a mutual listening in which everyone has something to learn. Faithful people, the College of Bishops, the Bishop of Rome: we are one in listening to others; and all are listening to the Holy Spirit, the 'spirit of truth' (Jn 14:17), to know what the Spirit 'is saying to the Churches' (Rv 2:7)."[45]

Various structures and levels of synodality exist within the church. At the level of the particular church or diocese, there are diocesan synods, presbyteral councils, colleges of consultors, and pastoral councils. At the level of ecclesiastical provinces and ecclesiastical regions, there are particular councils and conferences of bishops. The Plenary Councils of Baltimore (1852, 1866, 1884), the third of which gave us the Baltimore Catechism, is an example of a particular council, and the United States Conference of Catholic Bishops is an example of a conference of bishops. At the level of the church universal, there is the Synod of Bishops established by Paul VI in 1965.[46]

Pope Francis's convening of universal synods—the Synods on Marriage and the Family (2014), Synod on Young People (2018), Synod on the Church in the Pan-Amazon Region (2019), Synod on Synodality (2024)—emphasizes a new way of being in the church at every level. Walking together in synodality is meant to be the constitutive way of being church today, a process which should inform the church's ordinary way of living and working.[47]

Dialogue occurs at many levels and stages of a synod, and consultation can assume different modalities. Dialogue begins with the publication of the first document, the *Lineamenta* (the Latin term for outline), which introduces the topic of the synod and poses questions to generate discussion. Next, episcopal conferences are invited to offer responses to the *Lineamenta*. This is then followed by conversation between the general secretariat and the council of the general secretariat, which results in the production of the *Instrumentum Laboris*, the working paper for the synod. This, once approved by the pope, is made public and is sent to the delegates. A fourth set of preparatory conversations then occurs between bishops and their consultors or within episcopal conferences, at which stage the bishops can once again submit written responses. The relator of the assembly (more than one if there is more than one main topic at a given assembly) moderates and facilitates the synod dialogue and tries to foster consensus of the assembly. He prepares a third document which summarizes the *Instrumentum Laboris*, and written responses to it are received from episcopal conferences and individual bishops. This is sent out at least thirty days before the synod. When the synod convenes, the relator summarizes his report (*Relatio ante Disceptationem*).[48]

During the synod, procedures for dialogue have varied. Under John Paul II, during the first two weeks of the synod each bishop, as an individual or as a representative of an episcopal conference, could address the entire synod assembly for eight minutes on the topic of the synod with no follow-up dialogue allowed. If speaking on behalf of his conference, a bishop had to give both the majority and minority opinions of the conference.[49] This procedure was modified for the 2005 synod on "The Eucharist: Source and Summit of the Life and Mission of the Church" by Benedict XVI, who limited each bishop delegate to six-minute presentations to allow for an hour of free addresses by the participants at the end of the day.[50] These statements were synthesized in a fourth document, the *Relatio post Disceptationem*, as a basis for further discussion. Because these presentations were often prepared well in advance of the synod and were given in a sequence unrelated to each other, with no response, this initial process was far from being dialogical. Beginning in 1969, a first major set of conversations took place for a week in smaller language groups (*circuli minores*). The proposals or recommendations arising from there were gathered into a fifth document for consideration by the members of a drafting committee, who then prepared a sixth document in which they selected, combined, and edited the material from the language groups. This set of recommendations were then submitted to the entire assembly for debate and vote, a two-thirds majority being required for acceptance. In the final days of the synod, a seventh document, a final report, was prepared. However, beginning with 1974, when the bishops were unable to come to an agreement on a document on evangelization, the bishops submitted a list of recommendations and proposals to the pope and that practice continued in subsequent synods. About a year after the synod, the pope issues a ninth synod document, a post-synodal apostolic exhortation.

While the synods of bishops have been a welcome collegial structure in the church, both theological and practical concerns have been voiced. The major theological questions revolve around the collegial character and authority of the synod in relation to papal authority since the pope must receive the results of the synod and it is he who authors and promulgates the apostolic exhortation following the synod. Synods have been consultative to the pope rather than a deliberative authority. The primary practical concerns center on the limitations placed on dialogue in terms of adequate opportunity for dialogue and restrictions placed on topics that could be raised. A second practical concern centers on the process through which recommendations are finalized and brought forward to the synod assembly for vote. Bradford Hinze, in comparing the synodal process to the process of Vatican II that produced documents debated and refined by the council, views the move from a final report of the synod to a list of proposal and recommendations as "a diminishment of the role of dialogical discernment and decision-making exercised by the synod of bishops."[51] In his opinion, this avoids "the harder task of sharpening contested issues, confronting conflicts, and negotiating agreements with representatives of different positions."[52] Complaints about the process include the control by the Roman curia of the proceedings, the censorship of topics by ignoring or filtering out recommendations, and the editing and softening of recommendations in the interest of maximizing affirmative votes.[53]

The Synod on Synodality represented an effort to address some of these concerns, for the synod process itself was designed to be dialogical. The *Instrumentum Laboris* identifies "conversation in the Spirit" as the way of proceeding.[54] The goal is not just an exchange of ideas but is "a dynamic in which the word spoken and heard generates familiarity, enabling the participants to draw closer to one another."[55] To accomplish this, the synod alternated between plenary sessions (*Congregationes Generales*) and small working groups (*Circuli Minores*) as foreseen in Francis's Apostolic Constitution, *Episcopalis Communio*.[56] The latter groups employed a method of conversation in the Spirit in which, first, each person takes the floor and speaks from his or her experience as reread during the period of preparation and prayer on a topic outlined on a worksheet. Second, after a period of prayer and silence, each person again takes the floor, to express what has touched them most deeply and what they feel challenged by most strongly in what they heard in the first round of sharing. This was not a time to react or counter what they heard or to reaffirm their own position. Third, the group identifies the key points that emerged and builds a consensus on the fruits of the joint work.[57] This method of proceeding represents a sea change from earlier synodal procedures and models a synodal way of being church through active listening, intentional speaking in a prayerful context that builds communion and ensures participation, all for the sake of mission.

A synodal way of being church, however, is much more than any particular synod in the life of the church. Dialogue is the way of proceeding in a synodal way within all of the church's structures, from parish and pastoral councils to diocesan synods, to episcopal conferences, to the

Synod of Bishops. In fact, a synodal way of proceeding is likely most effective in a decentralized church at local levels because a broader participation is then possible and occurs closer to the implementation of the results.

Synodal consultation in the church takes place within a hierarchically structured community through a joint exercise of consultation, discernment, and cooperation. It does not supplant the role of the bishop, whose competence is to make a final decision. As the document *Synodality in the Life and Mission of the Church* affirms, "Working things out is a synodal task; decision is a ministerial responsibility."[58] Nevertheless, such consultation embodies the shared responsibility of everyone in the church and carries out maxim, "*Quod omnes tangit ab omnibus, tractari et approbari debet*" ("What concerns all must be discussed and approved by all").[59]

Dialogue does not take the place of the authority of bishops and pastors, but it can and should be a normal process within the church to assist those in authority to make good decisions. As a means of consulting the sense of the faith (*sensus fidei*) of the church, dialogue is one means of listening to the movement and inspiration of the Holy Spirit in the church. Dialogue is essential to the consultative process of decision-making by those who discern prior to the deliberative process of decision-taking by the appropriate authority.[60]

Within a synodal process, it is imperative that dialogue be conducted in an atmosphere of freedom, where a diversity of voices and competencies is represented and where a difference of opinions can be respectfully and patiently heard. Such inclusivity precludes the exclusive appointment of *pro forma* representatives of a particular faction in the church so that those in authority only hear what they want to hear or that only those with a particular axe to grind are represented. As Rahner expresses it, the Spirit "makes us bold enough to preserve continuity with our historical heritage, and at the same time daring enough to make new experiments even when these have not yet proved themselves."[61]

DIALOGUE WITH THE WORLD, CULTURE, AND OTHER FAITH TRADITIONS

The Second Vatican Council called for dialogue with separated Christians,[62] with non-Christians and atheists,[63] with the entire human family, and with the world.[64] Such a dialogue is not simply an altruistic goal motivated by pious convictions. Rahner argues that because today in a pluralistic society, people with diverse views occupy the same historical space and must therefore confront one another out of necessity, dialogue becomes the only possible mode of coexistence.[65] Dialogue in a pluralistic society is not an option, but a necessity. It can, however, be done well or badly.

Before the end of the council, Pope Paul VI in his 1964 encyclical, *Ecclesiam Suam*, said, "The Church should enter into dialogue with the world in which it exists and labors. The Church has something to say; the Church has a message to deliver; the Church has a communication to offer" (*ES* 67). The relationship with God in dialogue becomes the model for the relationship of the church to the human race in dialogue.[66] The church takes the initiative for dialogue (*ES* 74), it is motivated by love (*ES* 75), it is not proportioned to the merits of those who receive it (*ES* 76), it is not coercive (*ES* 77), it includes everyone (*ES* 78), it develops gradually taking into account psychological and historical maturation (*ES* 79), it is adapted to the nature of the interlocutor and to factual circumstances (*ES* 80), and excludes a priori condemnation and offensive polemics (*ES* 81). This dialogue does not aim at effecting the immediate conversion of the interlocuter, but aims at helping him and encouraging a fuller sharing of sentiments and convictions (*ES* 81).

Pope Francis, in *Evangelii Gaudium*, develops a theology of dialogue as intrinsic to the task of evangelization and the pursuit of peace. He identifies three areas of dialogue in which the church must engage in order to promote full human development and to pursue the common good: dialogue with states, dialogue with society—including dialogue with cultures and the sciences—and dialogue with other believers who are not part of the Catholic Church (*EG* 238). Francis identifies dialogue as "a means for building consensus and agreement while seeking the goal of a just, responsive and inclusive society" (*EG* 239). The church does not engage in this dialogue with ready-made solutions for every particular issue (*EG* 240), so her approach must be one of humility. In the dialogue with science, the path is one of a synthesis between "the responsible use of methods proper to the empirical sciences and other areas of knowledge such as philosophy, theology, as well as faith itself" (*EG* 242).

CONCLUSION

Dialogue carefully treads its way through several pitfalls and conundrums. First, dialogue can never be an exercise in reducing the matter at hand to the lowest common denominator. Second, while we are steadfast in our own convictions, dialogue must remain free of any coercion or force. Yet, these raise questions. Is dialogue that seeks to enlighten and convince the other without force really a dialogue, or is it preaching and propaganda? Or, if we abstain from convincing another, is the conversation contrary to a worldview that makes absolute and universal truth claims?[67] Is dialogue then simply an exchange of opinions? Is it simply wanting to get along with another? Is it then worthwhile? In any dialogue, but certainly in interreligious dialogue, as Pope Francis notes, "true openness involves remaining steadfast in one's deepest convictions, clear and joyful in one's own identity, while at the same time being 'open to understanding those of the other party' and 'knowing that dialogue can enrich each side'" (*EG* 251).

Dialogue is an attempt to understand the experience of the partner, his or her viewpoint, and the historical and affective experiences that have formed their position. Even absolute viewpoints are in some measure "on the way" as this viewpoint must always be reinterpreted and understood anew in evolving contexts. Furthermore, even if there is an unbridgeable gap between positions, this does not preclude building a relationship between persons, nor does it obviate the need to work together on common projects. This relationship with another different from ourselves contains something of the ineffable since if we in some ways remain mysteries to ourselves, so, too, this is true of those with whom we dialogue and thus one to the other. Dialogue not only attempts to discover and express a mutual truth; it also attempts to discern what is present in the depth of the heart.

Such dialogue cultivates a culture of encounter. Encounters engender relationships. Relationships create community. Community is built on mutual respect and love. Dialogue images the conversation of the disciples on the road to Emmaus, who recount the wonders that the Lord has worked during a journey that culminates in the shared recognition of the Lord in the breaking of the bread at a common table. This encounter and dialogue led to communion and resulted in a missionary dynamism as the two disciples returned to Jerusalem to announce that the Lord was risen (Lk 24:13–35). In dialogue, we have not yet reached the end of that journey of recognition, communion, and mission. Nor has the last word been uttered. And so that journey and the dialogue, continues.

NOTES

1. Paul VI, Encyclical *Ecclesiam Suam*, August 6, 1964, §83, https://www.vatican.va/content/paul-vi/en/encyclicals/documents/hf_p-vi_enc_06081964_ecclesiam.html. Hereafter *ES*.

2. Francis, "Meeting with Brazil's Leaders of Society," Apostolic Journey to Rio de Janeiro on the Occasion of the XXVIII World Youth Day, July 27, 2013, https://www.vatican.va/content/francesco/en/speeches/2013/july/documents/papa-francesco_20130727_gmg-classe-dirigente-rio.html.

3. Paul VI, Motu Proprio *Apostolica Sollicitudo*.

4. Hermann J. Pottmeyer, "Dialogue as Model for Communication in the Church," in *The Church and Communication*, ed. Patrick Granfield (New York: Sheed and Ward, 1994), 97–103, at 97. Karl Rahner makes a similar claim in "Dialogue within a Pluralist Society," in *Theological Investigations*, vol. 6 (Baltimore: Helicon Press, 1969), 31–42, at 34.

5. Francis, *Let Us Dream: The Path to a Better Future* (New York: Simon & Schuster, 2020), 85.

6. Paul VI, *ES* §90.

7. Instructions on active listening taken from Jesuits of Canada, *Communal Apostolic Discernment: A Toolkit*, November 2020, 6–8, https://www.christianlifecommunity.ca/wordpress/wp-content/uploads/2020/11/Comm_Discern_Toolkit_ENG_FINAL_web4_compressed-1-2.pdf.

8. Francis, Homily at the Occasion of the Opening of the Synodal Path (October 10, 2021), https://www.vatican.va/content/francesco/en/homilies/2021/documents/20211010-omelia-sinodo-vescovi.html.

9. Jos Moons, SJ, "A Comprehensive Introduction to Synodality: Reconfiguring Ecclesiology and Ecclesial Practice," *Roczniki Theologiczne* 69, no. 2 (2022): 74–93, at 86.

10. "Greeting of Pope Francis to the Synod Fathers during the First General Congregation of the Third Extraordinary General Assembly of the Synod of Bishops," October 6, 2014, https://www.vatican.va/content/francesco/en/speeches/2024/october/documents/papa-francesco_20241006_padri-sinodali.html.

11. Paul VI, *ES*, §§83–84.

12. Jesuits of Canada, *Communal Apostolic Discernment*, 8.

13. Eugenio Scalfari, "The Pope: How the Church Will Change," *La Repubblica*, October 1, 2013, https://www.repubblica.it/cultura/2013/10/01/news/pope_s_conversation_with_scalfari_english-67643118/.

14. Margaret O'Gara, *The Ecumenical Gift Exchange* (Collegeville, MN: Liturgical Press, 1998), vii, referring to John Paul II, *Ut unum sint*, *Origins* 25 (1995–1996): 49, 51–72.

15. Francis, *EG*, §20.

16. Francis, *EG* §236.

17. Karl Rahner raises this question in "Dialogue in the Church," in *Theological Investigations*, vol. 10 (New York: Herder and Herder, 1973), 103–21, at 104. Hereafter *TI*.

18. Paul VI, *ES*, §72.

19. Karl Rahner, *Hearers of the Word*, trans. Michael Richards (New York: Herder and Herder, 1969).

20. Council of Trent, Session 4, April 8, 1546, *Decrees of the Ecumenical Councils*, vol. 2, trans. and ed. Norman P Tanner, SJ (Washington, DC: Georgetown University Press, 1990), 664. Emphasis added.

21. See, for example, St. Ephraim the Syrian, "Perfectly God, he entered the womb through her ear"; and Jacob of Serug and, in the early seventh century, Venatius Fortunas. *Orthodox Christianity Then and Now*, March 2017, https://www.johnsanidopoulos.com/2017/03/the-conception-of-christ-through-ear-of.html.

22. Paul A. Soukup, *Communication and Theology: Introduction and Review of the Literature* (London: World Association for Communication and Culture, 1983), 51.

A Culture of Dialogue 113

23. See Wood, *One Baptism*, 157.
24. Vatican I, Dogmatic Constitution on the Catholic Faith (*Dei Filius*), chapter 2, "On Revelation" and chapter 3, "On Faith," in *Decrees of the Ecumenical Councils*, ed. Norman Tanner, SJ (New York: Sheed & Ward and Georgetown University Press), 806–7.
25. *Catechism of the Catholic Church* (Collegeville, MN: Liturgical Press, 1994), §142.
26. Ibid., §§142–43.
27. Ibid., §150.
28. "*Quidquid recipitur ad modum recipientis reciptiur.*" Thomas Aquinas, *Summa Theologiae*, Blackfriars edition (New York: McGraw-Hill, 1964), 1a, q. 12, a. 4.
29. Joseph Ratzinger, "Chapter II: The Transmission of Divine Revelation," in *Commentary on the Documents of Vatican II*, vol. 3, ed. Herbert Vorgrimler (New York: Herder and Herder, 1969), 196.
30. Vatican II, *LG* §12; see ITC, "*Sensus Fidei* in the Life of the Church," June 10, 2014, §49, https://www.vatican.va/roman_curia/congregations/cfaith/cti_documents/rc_cti_20140610_sensus-fidei_en.html#1._The_sensus_fidei_as_an_instinct_of_faith.
31. ITC, "*Sensus Fidei* in the Life of the Church," §72.
32. Ibid.
33. The council did not actually use the term *sensus fidelium*, but rather the term *sensus fidei*, the sense or instinct of faith given to all the baptized. For a history of the concept see John Burkhard, *The "Sense of the Faith" in History: Its Sources, Reception, and Theology* (Collegeville, MN: Liturgical Press, 2022).
34. Richard R. Gaillardetz, *Teaching with Authority: A Theology of the Magisterium in the Church* (Collegeville, MN: Liturgical Press, 1997), 228. See also Alois Grillmeier, "Konzil und Rezeption: Methodische Bemerkungen zu einem Thema der ökumenischen Diskussion der Gegenwart," *Theologie und Philosophie* 45 (1970): 321–522; Yves Congar, "La 'réception' comme réalité ecclésiologique," *Revue des sciences philosophiques et théologiques* 56 (1972): 369–403; Thomas Rausch, "Reception Past and Present," *Theological Studies* 47 (1986): 497–508; and Edward Kilmartin, "Reception in History: An Ecclesiological Phenomenon and Its Significance," *Journal of Ecumenical Studies* 21 (1984): 34–54.
35. Richard R. Gaillardetz, *Teaching with Authority*, 235.
36. Walter Kasper, "The Continuing Challenge of the Second Vatican Council: The Hermeneutics of the Conciliar Statements," in *Theology and Church* (New York: Crossroad, 1989), 166–76.
37. Hermann J. Pottmeyer, "A New Phase in the Reception of Vatican II," in *The Reception of Vatican II*, ed. Giuseppe Alberigo, Jean Pierre Jossua, and Joseph A. Komonchak (Washington, DC: Catholic University of America Press, 1987), 27–43.
38. This is a similar approach to that of Pope Francis for whom the poles of a dialectic do not resolve into a synthesis. His use of dialectic is influenced by Romano Guardini (*Gegansatz*, Matthias Grunewald, 1925) and Gaston Fessard (*La Dialectique des "Exercices spirituels" de saint Ignace de Loyola*, Aubier, 1956). See Massimo Borghesi, "The Polarity Model: The Influence of Gaston Fessard and Romano Guardini on Jorge Mario Bergoglio," in *Discovering Pope Francis: The Roots*

of Jorge Mario Bergoglio's Thinking, ed. Brian Y. Lee (Collegeville, MN: Liturgical Press, 2019), 93–113.

39. See Yves Congar, "Reception as an Ecclesiological Reality," in *Election and Consensus in the Church*, ed. G. Alberigo and A. Weiler, *Concilium* 77 (1972): 43–68, at 62.
40. Ibid., 64. Emphasis in original.
41. Soukup, *Communication and Theology*, 50.
42. Pottmeyer, "Dialogue as Model for Communication in the Church," 98.
43. Ibid.
44. Vatican II, *Ad Gentes*, §2.
45. Address of His Holiness Pope Francis, Ceremony Commemorating the 50th Anniversary of the Institution of the Synod of Bishops.
46. Paul VI , *Apostolica Sollicitudo*.
47. ITC, *Synodality in the Life and Mission of the Church*, 70a.
48. For these procedures I am indebted to Bradford Hinze, who gives a more detailed account of the process in *Practices of Dialogue in the Roman Catholic Church: Aims and Obstacles, Lessons and Laments* (New York: Continuum, 2006), 157–66. See also Thomas J. Reese, *Inside the Vatican: The Politics and Organization of the Catholic Church* (Cambridge, MA: Harvard University Press, 1996), 42–65; Synod of Bishops, "Synodal Information," March 9, 2005, https://www.vatican.va/roman_curia/synod/documents/rc_synod_20050309_documentation-profile_en.html; and Francis, Apostolic Constitution *Episcopalis Communio*, September 15, 2018, https://www.vatican.va/content/francesco/en/apost_constitutions/documents/papa-francesco_costituzione-ap_20180915_episcopalis-communio.html.
49. *Ordo Synodi Episcoporum Celebrandae*, "Synodal Information," D. "Certain explanations on the order of the Synod of Bishops; Re.: Article 23: The Manner of Seeking an Opinion," 22, cited by Hinze, *Practices of Dialogue in the Roman Catholic Church*, 164.
50. Hinze, *Practices of Dialogue*, 303, n. 25.
51. Ibid., 174.
52. Ibid., 176.
53. Ibid.
54. *IL*, First Session, §15, 32–42.
55. Ibid., §33.
56. Francis, *Episcopalis Communio*, §14.
57. *IL*, First Session, §§37–39.
58. ITC, *Synodality in the Life and Mission of the Church*, 69.
59. For a history of the phrase, see Yves M.-J. Congar, "*Quod omnes tangit ab omnibus, tractari et approbari debet*," *Revue historique de droit français et étranger (1922–)*, Quatrième série, 35 (1958): 210–59. For its use in canon law, see P. Landau, "The Origin of the Regula iuris 'Quod omnes tangit' in the Anglo-Norman School of Canon Law during the Twelfth Century," *Bulletin of Medieval Canon Law* 32 (May 15, 2016), https://muse.jhu.edu/article/618145.
60. Synod of Bishops, "Preparatory Document," Synod 2021–2023 (2021), 37, https://www.usccb.org/resources/synod-preparatory-document.
61. Rahner, "Dialogue in the Church," 114.

62. Vatican II, *UR,* §§9, 14, 18, 19, 21.
63. Vatican II, *GS* §§21, 92.
64. Vatican II, *GS* §§3, 20.
65. Vatican II, *GS* §35.
66. Paul VI, *ES* §73.
67. Questions raised by Karl Rahner in "Dialogue within a Pluralistic Society," *Theological Investigations* 6, trans. Karl–H. and Boniface Kruger (Baltimore: Helicon Press, 1969), 31–42, at 33.

6

Beyond Dialogue
Discernment in Common

A synodal church is a discerning church. Active listening and intentional speaking are essential components of discernment in common, but they are not yet discernment. "Discernment" is a term that is often used rather loosely and bantered about as roughly being the equivalent of "deciding," even if used in a context of prayer, whether by an individual or by a group. Discernment may be an activity of an individual or a group. Communal discernment[1] is not an exercise in democratic rule even though it is broadly participatory. A procedural democracy, where everyone has a voice and the voice of the majority rules, is not the same as discernment.[2] It is also more than group decision-making at a meeting that may begin with a prayer to the Holy Spirit. Its purpose, moreover, is not just to arrive at a sensible, expedient, or popular decision. After all, the wisdom of the cross is considered by some to be either madness or foolishness (1 Cor 1:18ff).[3] Finally, discernment is not the same thing as deliberation.

Communal discernment is a process that enables a group "to be aware of, to invoke and to respond faithfully to the presence and movement of the Spirit of God, and thus to 'find God's will.'"[4] The various components of discernment—prayer for the guidance of the Spirit, gathering the data, spiritual conversation, attention to the interior movements of desolation and consolation, reading the collective experience of the group—are all oriented to this objective. Discernment, an activity that should be undertaken by the community as a whole, is integral to mission as the church sifts through those things from which it needs to be purified and those things that need reform. Not only directed to the internal life of the church, discernment also incorporates an analysis of contemporary reality, a reading of the "signs of the time," so that the church may better fulfill its mission in the world.

Discernment has been a key theme in the pontificate of Pope Francis, a Jesuit with the Ignatian heritage of discernment in his DNA from his experience of the *Spiritual Exercises* of Ignatius of Loyola.[5] Francis's advocacy of ecclesial discernment was highlighted in *Evangelii Gaudium*, the apostolic exhortation which presented the orientation of his papacy. There he stressed, "To make this missionary impulse ever more focused, generous and fruitful, I encourage each particular Church to undertake a resolute process of discernment, purification and reform" (*EG* 30). Again, in a meeting with the Polish Jesuits in Krakow he told them, "the church needs to grow in discernment, in the capacity to discern."[6] He highlighted discernment in connection with ecclesial synodality, building a process of communal discernment into the proceedings of the 2021–2024 Synod on Synodality.

WHAT IS DISCERNMENT?

The term "discernment of spirits" was first used by Paul in his list of the variety of gifts in the Spirit (1 Cor 12:10). In 1 Thessalonians 5:19–20, he tells the community, "Do not quench the Spirit. Do not despise the words of prophets, but test everything." Discernment is a testing of a potential judgment or action.

Communal discernment is a Spirit-inspired human activity employed by a faith community seeking to find the will of God in a corporate decision to be taken. The process of discerning is an instrument used by the Holy Spirit to enable a group to recognize the will of God in a particular corporate decision. Luke Timothy Johnson, in his study of discernment in scripture, defines it "as that habit of faith by which we are properly disposed to hear God's Word, and properly disposed to respond to that Word in the practical circumstances of our lives."[7] John C. Futrell, SJ, describes discernment as a "conception, which involves choosing the way of the light of Christ instead of the way of the darkness of the Evil One and living out the consequences of this choice through discerning what specific decisions and actions are demanded to follow Christ here and now."[8] He identifies the goal of discernment as arriving "at the choice of authentic Christian response to the word of God in each concrete situation in life."[9] While these definitions can apply to either individual discernment or communal discernment, Jules J. Toner defines communal discernment as "a process undertaken by a community as a community for the purpose of judging what God is calling that community to do."[10] Pulling from these definitions, the elements of discernment include: (1) a habit of faith; (2) a deep listening to the word of God; (3) being in dialogue with the heritage of the tradition; (4) a concrete choice to be made; (5) a need to distinguish between light and darkness, the good from what is less good or perhaps even evil; (6) the motive to follow Christ in present concrete circumstances rather than a motive exterior to faith such as greater comfort or financial profit; (7) a conviction that God speaks to us through the concrete realities of our experiences and that we are called to respond; and (8) judgment and commitment to action.

Discernment is more of a process than it is a "recipe" or "algebraic method" for arriving at a solution to a problem. Neither is it a sophisticated process or a mental activity reserved to those who are wise or especially knowledgeable. Diego Fares describes it as "the capacity of the simple and little ones to recognize the 'moment of grace' in which God is in the process of working."[11]

A great interest in communal discernment occurred in the wake of the Second Vatican Council in the late 1960s and 1970s when religious communities were mandated to revise their constitutions in the light of *Perfectae Caritatis,* The Decree on Religious Life.[12] Some religious communities used communal discernment to reclaim the charisms of their founders, to reexamine their mission, and to align their way of living to this mission. This occasioned significant publications on the topic.[13] More recently, communal discernment is once again receiving considerable attention as an important component of synodal processes encouraged by Pope Francis and modeled by the Synod on Synodality.

DISCERNMENT IN COMMON: FOUR EXAMPLES

Many Christian groups have used processes for communal decision-making. Although the details of these processes vary, similarities can be found in terms of the presupposition that the Holy Spirit is at work in the process, that consultation and listening by those in authority assist them in making a good decision, and that confirmation of a decision occurs in experiences of consolation and the good fruits that follow. Four examples illustrate discernment in common as practiced by various Christian groups: the Apostolic Council of Jerusalem in the first century, Benedictine monasticism, the Society of Friends (Quakers), and the first Jesuits.

The Apostolic Council of Jerusalem

The biblical precedent for discernment in common in the New Testament is found in the Apostolic Council of Jerusalem (c. 48–50 AD) as recounted in Acts 16:2–35. The council was occasioned by the debate on whether

Gentile Christians had to observe the Mosaic Law of the Jews requiring circumcision and observance of dietary laws. Paul and Barnabas were appointed to go to Jerusalem and discuss the matter with the apostles and the elders. The conference, led by Peter and James, determined that Gentile Christians were not bound by the Levitical regulations except for abstention "from things polluted by idols and from fornication and from whatever has been strangled and from blood" (Acts 15:19).[14]

Notably, this conference was occasioned by a concrete decision that had to be made. The matter occasioned debate as there was "no small dissension" on the matter. It was determined that Paul and Barnabas discuss this with the apostles and elders. The data was reviewed, which included "all the signs and wonders that God had done through them among the Gentiles" (Acts 15:12) and the fact that God had looked favorably upon the Gentiles by taking from among them "a people for his name" (Acts 15:14). The data was interpreted in the light of the received faith tradition of the prophets (Acts 15:16–18). A decision was made by Peter in his capacity as a "Pillar of the Church." The decision was disseminated by sending Paul and Barnabas with others back to Antioch to attest in person the contents of the letter they brought communicating the decision. Significantly, the letter states, "For it has seemed good to the Holy Spirit and to us to impose on you no further burden than these essentials" (Acts 15:28). This attests to their belief that the Holy Spirit was at work in the process of consultation, review of data, the evaluation of the data in terms of the faith tradition, and the decision.

Benedictine Monasticism

Benedictine monasticism is well known for the role of the community chapter in assisting the abbot to make good decisions. The Prologue to the Rule of Benedict emphasizes listening: "Listen carefully, my child to your master's precepts and incline the ear of your heart" (Prv 4:20). There is a kind of listening that can only be done with the ears of the heart, so listening extends beyond external words and superficial meanings. The abbot must consult the whole community:

> Whenever any important business has to be done in the monastery let the Abbot call together the whole community and state the matter to be acted upon. Then, having heard the brethren's advice, let him turn the matter over in his own mind and do what he shall judge to be most expedient. The reason we have said that all should be called for counsel is that the Lord often reveals to the youngest what is best.[15]

Monastic listening requires humility because the proud think they already know everything, exterior and interior silence to allow the monk to hear with both mind and heart, and obedience because listening and discernment lead to decisions resulting in action.

The Benedictine contributions to communal discernment include the recognition that listening is deeper than hearing words, because one must also listen with heart and supposedly also to the heart of another. All are consulted with special attention given to the youngest, so there is an egalitarianism in listening to the voices of the community. There is a concrete matter at hand to be discerned. As with the Council of Jerusalem, the leader of the community makes the final decision after weighing what he has heard. Finally, the discernment is related to the lifestyle and virtues of monastic life.

The Religious Society of Friends (Quakers)

Discernment is an activity that characterizes a wide array of Christian traditions. The Religious Society of Friends (Quakers) follows its own unique method of communal decision-making based on discernment.[16] Friends seek the "sense of the meeting" that can transcend individual preferences through a process of communal discernment that does not involve voting. It is based on the insights of George Fox and the early Friends that each individual is directly open to the power of the Spirit and that the gathered community is needed for support and encouragement when ideas are tested. This gathered experience of the Spirit is an egalitarian and nonhierarchical process that goes beyond consensus. The goal is unity in the Spirit for decision-making even if this takes time despite the urgency of the business. The process must take as long as it needs. All those participating need not agree, but a "sense of the meeting" can emerge as a way forward for the group at that time. Strengths of this process include ownership by the whole group, the spiritual authority of the decisions derived from the process of arriving at it together, and the sense of unity within the group. Decisions are still subject to error, resulting in the need for further subsequent discernment using the same process.

The contributions to communal discernment by the Society of Friends include a strong pneumatological spirituality and belief in the guidance of the Holy Spirit. The Friends employ a process in which each individual speaks his or her truth as they see it without discussion or argument. The group seeks the "sense of the meeting" with the realization that not all may agree with the decision even while they agree on the "sense of the meeting," with dissenting individuals bowing to the sense of the group. As with the Benedictine model, the listening process is egalitarian. Importantly, there is a realization that discernment takes time and should not be rushed. This is an important learning as communal discernment is applied to various ecclesial situations that may risk a utilitarian approach with an expectation of quick results.

The First Members of the Society of Jesus

The practice of discernment in common in Jesuit usage is generally traced to the *Deliberatio primorum partum,* an account of the deliberations by Ignatius Loyola and his companions in Rome in 1539 that led to the formation of the Society of Jesus.[17] Not yet a religious order, a group of priests bonded by their love for Jesus Christ, their dedication to apostolic work under the authority of the pope, and their adherence to the leadership of Ignatius faced a dilemma about their future when the pope wanted to disperse them all over Europe in response to the requests of bishops. They came together in 1539 to discern God's will for them, that is, whether they should join together more formally and whether they should pronounce a third vow, a vow of obedience to one of their members.[18] They devised a method in which they gathered data on potential negative consequences of a vow of obedience and then on the next day the positive consequences, all done individually without communication with the others and all in the context of prayer. This was followed by many days of weighing the mass of data, again in a context of prayer. The group came to the unanimous judgment that obedience to one of the group was necessary to actualize their desire to fulfill God's will in all details of life, to preserve the Society, and to provide for their spiritual and temporal needs.[19]

THE THEOLOGICAL FOUNDATIONS OF DISCERNMENT

As was developed in the first chapter, baptism is the sacramental foundation of a synodal church and is the sacrament, along with confirmation, in which believers receive the indwelling of the Holy Spirit and the Spirit's gifts and charisms. Discernment is founded on the beliefs that (1) God works through people and human events, and one can get in touch with God's presence and activity by being in touch with one's interiority in connection with his activity in history as transmitted in the heritage of a faith tradition; and (2) each person receives gifts of the Spirit, enabling them to spiritually resonate with the action of the Holy Spirit. God works through human processes, so discernment does not bypass human activities such as dialogue and collection of data, but the theological foundations of discernment are found in the gifts of the Spirit evident in the process of discernment. These include charisms, the *sensus fidei* (sense of the faith) and the *sensus fidelium* (sense of the faithful), and *communio* (communion).

Charisms

Charisms are generally understood to be gifts of the Holy Spirit given to an individual for the upbuilding of the church (Eph 4:12). Gifts of the Spirit are forms of service to the community. Gifts of the Spirit listed in 1 Cor 12:8–10 are wisdom, the utterance of knowledge, faith, healing, the working of miracles, prophecy, the discernment of spirits, various kinds of tongues and the interpretation of tongues, although charisms are hardly to be limited to these. The test of a genuine charism is whether it contributes to the common good (1 Cor 12:7). The genuineness of a charism is judged by its effect (1 Cor 12:2). Paul gives two examples. The first negative example is being led astray to idols (1 Cor 12:2) and the second example is the assertion that "no one speaking by the Spirit of God ever says 'Let Jesus be cursed!' and no one can say 'Jesus is Lord' except by the Holy Spirit" (1 Cor 12:3).

Lumen Gentium, the Dogmatic Constitution on the Church from the Second Vatican Council, affirms that "the Spirit dwells in the Church and in the hearts of the faithful as in a temple" (*LG* 4) and that the church is equipped "with hierarchical and charismatic gifts" (*LG* 4). It picks up Paul's theology of charisms affirming that the faithful are endowed with charisms (*LG* 7), that the Spirit gives the body of the church unity (*LG* 7), and that the Spirit distributes graces among the faithful of every rank that enable them to undertake their various tasks and offices, which contribute toward the renewal and building up of the church (*LG* 12).

Pope Francis discusses charisms at the service of a communion which evangelizes in his Apostolic Exhortation *Evangelii Gaudium*.[20] Meant to build up and renew the church, charisms are "gifts of the Spirit integrated into the body of the Church" and "channeled into an evangelizing impulse" (*EG* 130). In other words, charisms serve the mission of the church and the heart of the Gospel, which for Francis is the proclamation of the tender mercy of God (*EG* 164). The authenticity and fruitfulness of a charism derive from its being exercised in communion. Thus, charisms are fundamentally ecclesial.

In this same section of *Evangelii Gaudium*, Pope Francis discusses the paradox that the Holy Spirit is both the source of diversity, plurality, and multiplicity and at the same time brings about unity (*EG* 131). Only when this diversity is reconciled by the Holy Spirit do we avoid being self-enclosed, exclusive, and divisive on one hand, or avoid imposing a monolithic uniformity on the other hand. The Holy Spirit enables a unity in diversity.

The theology of charisms in its biblical foundations and as reiterated by Vatican II and developed by Pope Francis contributes to a synodal church with the affirmation that all the baptized are endowed with charisms and that all are called to contribute to the church. This is even more reason why the faithful should be consulted by those making decisions on behalf of the church. It also provides a theological foundation for the active participation of the faithful in the life of the church as they exercise their charisms.

Sensus Fidei (Sense of the Faith) and *Sensus Fidelium* (Sense of the Faithful)

The *sensus fidei* (sense of the faith) and *sensus fidelium* (sense of the faithful) are two distinct but interrelated terms expressing the ability of the faithful to come to some knowledge or apprehension of matters of the faith through the assistance of the Holy Spirit. The term *sensus fidei* emphasizes the faith that is known while the second, the *sensus fidelium*, refers to the body of those who believe. *Lumen Gentium* 12 explains *sensus fidelium* as the sense of the universal body of the faithful:

> The whole body of the faithful who have received the anointing which comes from the holy one (see 1 Jn 2:20 and 27), cannot be mistaken in belief. It shows this characteristic through the entire people's supernatural sense of the faith when "from the bishops to the last of the faithful," it manifests a universal consensus in matters of faith and morals.

The text attributes to the *universal* body of the faithful, the *sensus fidei*, not just to the members of a particular church, not just to individuals, and not just to a particular group within the church such as a synod, a supernatural sense of the faith when this body expresses the consent (*consensum*) of all in matters of faith and morals. This body of the faithful "adheres indefectibly to the 'faith once for all delivered to the saints'" and "penetrates it more deeply into that same faith through right judgment and applies it more fully in daily life" (*LG* 12).

Turning now to the term *sensus fidei*, this expression refers to an instinct of faith which enables the faithful to discern what is truly of God (*EG* 119). The term *sensus fidei* has two parts. The first, *sensus*, refers to a particular type of knowledge and the second, *fidei*, refers to the object of that knowledge, that is, the faith. To begin with the latter, faith, one observes that the text from *Lumen gentium* 12 refers to faith in the singular as in "supernatural sense of the faith," and "penetrates more deeply into that same faith," but it also slips into a plurality where it speaks of "matters of faith and morals." We can ask, then, is the *sensus fidei* about all kinds of things that are to be believed, a plurality, or is faith unitary, a whole, a "one"?

The document from the International Theological Commission, "*Sensus Fidei* in the Life of the Church,"[21] speaks of faith as a response to the word of God, identified with the Gospel (§8). As the text notes, "The Gospel has a strong subject; Jesus himself, the word of God" (§9). Thus, faith is "both an act of belief or trust and also that which is believed or confessed, *fides qua* and *fides quae*" (§10). Obviously, the primary object of what is believed is the person of Christ, which suggests the dynamic within which a *sensus fidei* occurs. This dynamic must be one of dialogical encounter.

The *sensus fidei* begins with an encounter with the transformative love of Christ. Pope Francis in his Apostolic Exhortation *Evangelii Gaudium* echoes *Dei Verbum's* personalist understanding of divine disclosure in his invitation to all Christians to a renewed personal encounter with Jesus Christ (*EG* 3). He advocates a loving contemplation of the scriptures which we read with the heart (*EG* 264). He urges a personal transparency to Christ, a posture of an open heart and a reception of Jesus's gaze of love as when he told Nathaniel, "I saw you under the fig tree" (*EG* 262). This encounter is also an experience of God's mercy, and the fruit of this encounter is joy, the "joy of the Gospel." Since the *sensus fidei* is acquired through an encounter with Christ and through the activity of the Holy Spirit, this explains why prayer is essential to any process of discernment.

Fiduciary faith begins with this experience of encounter and return to the heart of the Gospel message. This encounter with Christ occurs in daily prayer, in the renewed study of the scriptures in the liturgical life of the church, and in service to the poor. This encounter with Christ is the source of both a universal and unitary faith, that which all the faithful share in common. The knowledge obtained through this experience is intellectual, involves a connaturality to grace, and involves the whole person, including the will.

Turning now to the other term in *sensus fidei*, namely *sensus,* I suggest that this refers to a specific kind of knowledge known as connatural knowledge. The term "connatural" is used to mean that from within the very core of the human person, at the fine point of the graced human spirit, at the place of deepest freedom and mystery, created grace recognizes and knows its source, the Creator. Like recognizes like, and that is the experience of unity and harmony that become the root of the experience of consolation in a process of discernment. This experience of consolation is the fundamental principle in Ignatius's method of supernatural logic by which every person makes decisions.

St. Thomas refers to connatural knowledge in his discussion on moral judgment. He distinguishes two different ways to make a moral judgment. In the first, we possess a conceptual and rational knowledge of virtues that produces in us an intellectual conformity with the truths involved. In the second instance, we possess the virtue in question in our own powers of will and desire, have it embodied in ourselves and are thus co-natured with it. In this second instance, when we are asked about a moral virtue, we give the right answer by looking at and consulting what we are and the inner bents or propensities of our own being.

St. Thomas illustrates these two types of judgments in his discussion on wisdom.[22] The person who possesses the science of morals judges rightly about matters of chastity, for example, after inquiring with his reason while the person who actually possesses the habit of chastity judges by a kind of connaturality. In the second instance, "it belongs to wisdom as a gift of the Holy Spirit to judge right about them on account of connaturality with them."[23] Furthermore, "this sympathy or connaturality for divine things is the result of charity which unites us to God."[24]

Connaturality, then, is possible only on account of the gift of the wisdom given on the initiative of God. As distinct from the other gifts, wisdom is knowledge of divine things through union, that is, through love. Since the cause of this wisdom is in the will, the will moves the intellect to judge rightly. The role of the will here contrasts wisdom with the other intellectual gifts in that wisdom is knowledge of divine things through taste and affective union. It is knowledge through union rather than through reason.

Jacques Maritain builds on Thomas, defining connaturality as affective and nonconceptual. It is a knowledge produced in the intellect, not by way of making conceptual connections but through inclination, "by looking at and consulting what we are and the inner bents or propensities of our being."[25] He says,

> In this knowledge through union or inclination, connaturality of congeniality, the intellect is at play not alone, but together with affective inclinations and the dispositions of the will, and is guided and directed by them. It is not rational knowledge, knowledge through the conceptual, logical and discursive exercise of reason. But it is really and genuinely knowledge, though obscure and perhaps incapable of giving account of itself, or of being translated into words.[26]

In another essay Maritain poetically observes that "the intellect in order to bear judgment, consults and listens to the inner melody that the vibrating strings of abiding tendencies made present in the subject."[27]

Connatural knowledge, particularly in its affective dimension, is an essential component of the discernment of spirits since it assists in the apprehension of consolation and desolation. In spite of its emotional dimension, however, Karl Rahner is careful to note that this experience is not reducible to "feeling," instinct, or something similar, contrary to or apart from the intellect. However, neither is it a cognition that is rationally discursive and conceptually expressible. It is, rather, "a thoroughly intellectual operation of the 'intellect,' in the metaphysical, scholastic sense of the word, in which it is capable of apprehending values."[28] Rational reflection is an indispensable element in the motion of spirits inasmuch as the motions themselves contain an objective conceptual element and can be expressed and verified and insofar as the experience of consolation and desolation is the result of impulses having a rational structure.[29]

Knowledge obtained through discernment is very much akin to the connatural knowledge, the knowledge obtained by affinity. St. Ignatius comments in the *Spiritual Exercises*, "For what fills and satisfies the soul consists, not in knowing much, but in our understanding the realities profoundly and in savoring them interiorly."[30] This knowledge is discovered, appropriated, and authenticated through consolations from God.[31]

This individual *sensus fidei* is related to a *consensus fidelium* insofar as the more authentic a personal experience, the more that experience resonates with other individual experiences and therefore is characterized as universal. The *sensus fidei* is mediated through the individual, but there is a reciprocal relationship between the individual and the communal insofar as the individual encountering the Gospel in faith encounters it as proclaimed to the people of God, within a community of faith constituted by the Spirit, and within a liturgy where the individual is constituted a member of the body of Christ.

Communio (Communion)

Communio (communion) is a theological foundation of communal discernment because we are considering discernment in common, the discernment of a group. Furthermore, communal discernment is not about the individual, but the community. Just as charisms given to individuals are for the upbuilding of the church, discernment in common builds on the discernment of individuals in order that the community may contribute to the reign of God by following the guidance of the Holy Spirit. *Communio* is a gift of the Spirit because the Holy Spirit is the bond of communion within the church, the bond of charity that unites believers. We go to God in communion with one another because, as *Lumen Gentium* asserts, "It has pleased God, however, to sanctify and save men and women not individually and without regard for what binds them together, but to set them up as a people who would acknowledge him in truth and serve him in holiness" (*LG* 9). Discernment in common proceeds from an experience of community and deepens it.

All the members of the community participate in communal discernment because all have an equal dignity due to their common baptism; all have been "made to drink of one Spirit" (1 Cor 12:13). In baptism, all are made into one body (Gal 3:28). This equality becomes a criterion of communal discernment insofar as judgment or decisions within the group either create privilege and elitism or call the group to a celebration of diversity and a variety of gifts.[32]

The Prerequisites for Discernment in Common

Prayer

A habit of prayer, inseparable from a habit of faith, is a necessary prerequisite for discernment, whether individual or communal. If discernment is a listening to the movements of the Holy Spirit, it goes without saying that one must have learned the "art" of this listening prior to an act of discernment. All writers on discernment share this conviction.[33]

Intense prayer during a formal period of discernment over several weekends or even throughout an intense month of a meeting of the Synod of Bishops does not take the place of long years of a habit of contemplation. Ladislas Orsy comments, "A habitually prayerful person will discern better in a short time than a dissipated one praying at length over the issue. . . . It is of some importance that discernment should be made in a prayerful framework; it is of greater importance that those who discern should be prayerful persons."[34] With respect to communal discernment he adds, "the more remote a person is from contemplative insight, the less he or she should presume that he or she is able to discover reliably the movement of grace in a community."[35]

Interior Freedom

Discernment requires interior freedom, what in Jesuit parlance is called "indifference." This does not mean that a person does not care about something or have an opinion about it. It does mean, however, that a person has opened up an interior space so that they are open to receiving a variety of views and experiences. They are free enough from their own prejudices and biases as well as pressures of public opinion and other influences to be open to the movement of the Spirit and whatever surprises may arise from the discernment process. "Indifference" is disregarding "any motivation for decision other than pure love for God" and "a single-hearted desire for his greater glory in self and in others."[36] A good decision requires that a group enter into the process either in a state of consolation or at least equilibrium, not being moved in one direction or another. Throughout the process, an individual must maintain his or her individual freedom and not fall under pressure to conform to the group so that there is no discordant note. Ladislas Orsy observes that this conforming to group pressure would be "all the more dangerous because it has the appearance of harmony."[37] Thus, a variety of opinions, judgments, can be expected to arise in the process of discernment.

Prior Personal Discernment

Even before prior personal discernment on the topic of a communal discernment, a habit of discernment and awareness of one's own freedoms and unfreedoms is necessary before one can listen actively or speak intentionally.[38] Within the Ignatian tradition, this awareness can be developed through the practice of a consciousness examen. This exercise usually consists of five steps: (1) prayer for enlightenment; (2) reflective thanksgiving for the day; (3) a survey of the subtle, affective ways that God has been acting in my life and my response; (4) contrition and sorrow for failings; and (5) hopeful resolution for the future.[39]

Before discerning communally, a person should have discerned individually. This means that the person will have studied the data on the decision to be made, have brought the matter to prayer, and have noted his or her own personal responses of consolation and desolation. Have they experienced peace, joy, love, wisdom, increased faith, and hope? Or is there lack of faith, hope, and love experienced in cynicism, turmoil, listlessness, tepidity? The first are associated with consolation, the second with desolation.

This personal discernment provides the basis of a person's intentional speaking in the process of discernment in common. As John Futrell indicates, "Communal discernment unites and brings together the individual spiritual experiences of the persons discerning as a community."[40] Thus, each person must reflect on the evidence, discerning the movements of their hearts. After this, the community as a whole must arrive at a shared experience of the movement of the Holy Spirit based on the sharing and listening of individuals, which may elicit new movements of the Holy Spirit that may enlighten the sharing of each individual and lead to a common discernment.

Identification of a Concrete Object of Discernment

Communal discernment is not a procedure for ordinary everyday governance but may be a helpful way of proceeding when a particular organization is at a crossroads or facing a particular important decision. As the superior general of the Society of Jesus, Adolfo Nicolás noted, "Discernment is never abstract; it is always about something concrete."[41] The proposal for discernment must be real and important. Pope Francis has said that "realities are greater than ideas."[42] This is based on the incarnational principle that Jesus Christ came in the flesh, that salvation occurs within history, that the Gospel is proclaimed and received within the particularities of culture, and that God is present in and is mediated through concrete events, persons, and experiences. Decisions and actions are discerned, not ideas or feelings, although affectivity is an important component in the discernment of decisions and actions. Pope Francis notes the tension between ideas and realities and the necessity of a continuous dialogue between the two (*EG* 231) but fears that ideas may become detached from reality, may mask reality, resulting in "angelic forms of purity, dictatorships of relativism, empty rhetoric, objectives more ideal than real, brands of ahistorical fundamentalism, ethical systems bereft of kindness, intellectual discourse bereft of wisdom" (*EG* 231). Discernment must necessarily concentrate on the concrete and the possible, avoiding the repetition of ideological slogans—be they liberal or conservative—and ideal aspirations inconsistent with the data at hand. Discernment seeks to recognize in the light of the Spirit "a call which God causes to resound in the historical situation itself" through which God calls the believer (*EG* 154). That which is to be discerned must be either "indifferent" or "good."[43] Something evil can never be an object of discernment. However, it bears noting that whether or not some object is "evil" or the label "sin" properly applies is at times contested territory. Some Christian groups are running into this with questions of LGBTQ+ Christians, while in the Catholic Church the controversy over *Fiducia Supplicans,* Francis's document regarding the blessing of individuals who are in irregular unions, raises protests that the church "cannot bless sin" even though individuals, not the union, is what is blessed.

A clear definition of the question at hand must be formulated in advance. The question must be formulated so that it is oriented to a particular concrete decision to be taken and must elicit a clear answer. The question is the subject of the discernment. The corporate decision must be both precise and executable.[44]

Adequate Data and Discerning Judgment

Discernment must be based upon adequate data. Discernment is not just how we feel about something without adequate information; it must be based on accurate data. This requires prior preparation both in the gathering of data, its dissemination, and its study by those who will discern. This data may be obtained from common sense or the experience of those discerning. An example here would be the first Jesuits listing all the reasons to support a vow of obedience and those reasons that might be counterindications of such a vow. It is also possible for data to come from the physical and social sciences and human experiences outside of the group discerning, particularly when it is a discernment of how to bring the Gospel message to different cultural contexts and groups. Yet, such data cannot be used indiscriminately, but must be subjected to critical thinking and evaluation.

Prayerful, spiritual discernment does not bypass the human processes of good decision-making, which includes the use of critical human intelligence applied to the information at hand. Even when decisions appear to be confirmed by the consolation of the group, outcomes may be influenced by narrowness of mind as well as by inordinate attachments of the heart.

The Right People at the Table

The discernment in common must have the participation of the right people for that particular decision. They must be free and capable of listening to the Spirit in their own lives. In addition, they must be acquainted with the relevant facts and have the necessary knowledge of the subject for discernment and the intelligence to engage in the topic at hand. While historically only bishops (and by default among Catholics only men, and for a long time predominantly Europeans) have been at the ecclesiastical table, today cultural, racial, and gender diversity is needed to discern for a worldwide church.

Clarity about Who Makes the Final Decision

There needs to be clarity from the very beginning of the discernment about who makes the final decision, which may not be the group that makes the discernment.[45] Depending on the authority structure of the group, the communal discernment might be provisional, dependent on the decision of the religious superior, the local bishop, or some other person with the responsibility for a final decision.

APPREHENSION OF CONSOLATION AND DESOLATION

Individuals and the group must be able to apprehend inner movements of consolation and desolation to ascertain whether a particular judgment or course of action is in harmony and resonates with the promptings of the Holy Spirit or whether it departs from them in an experience of dissonance, agitation, or discord. In communal discernment, the group itself becomes the subject of the spiritual movements of consolation and desolation, which are more than the sum total of the experiences of the individual members. As Jos Moons has observed, "In its Ignatian understanding, discernment is based on interiority and affectivity."[46] Unfortunately, the apprehension of consolation and desolation is not as simple as whether we feel good about a decision or feel bad about it. As Ladislas Orsy comments, "Consolations or desolations are signs of the disposition of a person before God. Since they are signs, and not reality itself, it is never easy to interpret them."[47]

St. Ignatius of Loyola describes consolation in the *Spiritual Exercises*, §§313–36., thus:

> By [this kind of] consolation I mean that which occurs when some interior motion is caused within the soul through which it comes to be inflamed with love of its Creator and Lord. As a result it can love no created thing on the face of the earth in itself, but only in the Creator of them all.
>
> Similarly, this consolation is experienced when the soul sheds tears which move it to love for its Lord—whether they are tears of grief for its own sins, or about the Passion of Christ our Lord, or about other matters directly ordered to his service and praise.
>
> Finally, under the word consolation I include every increase in hope, faith, and charity, and every interior joy which calls and attracts one toward heavenly things and to the salvation of one's soul, by bringing it tranquility and peace in its Creator and Lord.[48]

Some descriptors of communal consolation identified by the Canadian Jesuits include an increase of faith, hope, and love; a new sense of freedom; recognition of the talents within the group; ability to acknowledge and deal with obstacles; a new capacity for mutual listening; an apostolic thrust; a peaceful acceptance of reality; commitment to a discerned decision and its implementation.[49] Significantly, as Futrell notes, "the unanimity of profound peace which is the confirmation of the result of communal spiritual discernment is not the same thing as a unanimous opinion that the decision in itself is the best possible choice."[50] One may disagree with an outcome, but recognize and accept the discernment of the community as a whole.

On the other hand, St. Ignatius describes desolation as:

> obtuseness of soul, turmoil within it, an impulsive motion toward low and earthly things, or disquiet from various agitations and temptations. These move one toward lack of faith and leave one without hope and without love. One is completely listless, tepid, and unhappy, and feels separated from our Creator and Lord.
>
> For just as the consolation is contrary to desolation, so the thoughts which arise from consolation are likewise contrary to those which spring from desolation.[51]

Some descriptors of communal desolation identified by the Canadian Jesuits include fear as a predominant emotion. To this, one can add a preoccupation with personal agendas and old ineffectual ways of doing things, patterns of emotional dishonesty and refusal to give honest opinions, denial of the truth, unwillingness to face suffering, competition, avoidance of a required decision, manipulation and control tactics, signs of group disunity, feelings of hopelessness, hanging on to past hurts, an experience of the group being "stuck," unable to move forward, and expressions of a superiority of opinion.[52]

While generally the distinction between consolation and desolation is whether the interior experience is pleasurable or painful, this depends on whether or not a person is disposed toward the good or whether this person is inclined toward evil. A person inclined toward the good responds negatively to a movement issuing from an evil spirit with gnawing anxiety, sadness, restlessness, depression.[53] The opposite is true for a person given to evil. In this case, the person responds to evil suggestions with delight and pleasure. According to Ignatius, a person who is progressing from good to better in the service of God responds to the movement of the good spirit with courage and strength, consolations, tears, inspirations, and tranquillity.[54]

Yet additional differences distinguish consolation from desolation. John English, SJ, notes that spiritual consolation directs a person outward to other persons or the whole of humanity, while spiritual desolation "is an interior experience of movement of the affections into oneself alone, pleasurable as that might be at times."[55]

In addition to the apprehension of consolation or desolation, there can be other criteria applied to test a discernment. For instance, as Francis notes, "When Saint Paul approached the apostles in Jerusalem to discern whether he was 'running or had run in vain' (Gal 2:2), the key criterion of authenticity which they presented was that he should not forget the poor (cf. Gal 2:10)" (*EG* 195). This is a good example of what we call today the "option for the poor." Paul VI applied as a criterion to true development that it must be directed to all people and to the whole person.[56] Another principle of discernment would be how a particular decision contributes to the mission of a particular group or to the church as a whole. For a group embarking upon a process of communal discernment, it would be helpful to identify criteria such as these or others at the beginning of the process.

Procedures for Discernment in Common

Fundamentally, discernment is a process rather than a technique. It is not a "recipe" that one follows step by step, with the assurance of a guaranteed outcome at the end. Neither is it a process reserved to an educated elite or professionals. Simply put, even though detailed processes for discernment have been proposed, they can be reduced to three main components: (1) to feel and perceive the different motivations for acting, (2) to analyze them to see if they bring us closer or distance us from Gospel criteria, and (3) to act on the consequences of the analysis.[57] Basically, this is the "See, Judge, Act" method of analysis in Catholic Social Teaching or "Experience, Reflection, Action" method of Ignatian Pedagogy.[58]

Methods of Discernment in Common

There is no *one* model of communal discernment, and any model needs to be adapted both to the subject of the discernment and the group doing the discerning. In what follows, I will outline two methods for communal discernment, one by John Carroll Futrell[59] and the other outlined in the publication of the Canadian Jesuits, *Communal Apostolic Discernment: A Toolkit*.[60] The latter largely follows the methodology of ISECP (Ignatian Spiritual Exercises for the Corporate Person).[61]

The pattern for communal discernment outlined by John Futrell follows:

1. Prayer for light from the Holy Spirit
2. Each person reports from his or her personal discernment reasons against the proposed choice.
3. Brief break to reflect on the results of step 2.
4. Each person reports from his or her personal discernment, reasons in favor of the proposed choice. Here, determine whether it is immediately clear from the recorded pros and cons what the election should be. If this can be determined, go immediately to step 7.
5. Brief break to reflect on step 4 in the light of step 2.
6. Evaluate the weight of the reasons, con and pro, and then communally discern the choice to which the community is being called. This deliberation can proceed as an open discussion.
7. End with a prayer of thanksgiving and a corporate reaffirmation of the commitment to carry out the decision.[62]

The procedure for communal apostolic discernment developed by the Canadian Jesuits follows this pattern:[63]

1. Opening Prayer
2. The Check-In: all participants are invited to express how they are doing or feeling at the moment, the disposition they bring to the meeting.
3. First Round of Spiritual Conversation: Prior to the meeting, members of the group will have spent time in personal prayer with the matter under consideration for the meeting. In the first round of

spiritual conversation, each person shares something from that time of personal prayer. When everyone has shared, this is followed by a prayer pause.
4. Second Round of Spiritual Conversation: This round is in response to the first round. The participants are invited to share what they heard, what common themes arose, how they were emotionally affected by what they heard, what insights occurred to them, and where they experienced harmony with others.
5. Third Round: The purpose of this round is to arrive at a communal discernment. The participants are invited to identify communal consolations and/or desolations in the previous rounds. The leader summarizes them and then invites a discussion of what these might mean for the group. Hopefully, the group arrives at some agreement about both the identification and interpretation of some of these communal movements. Consensus does not mean unanimity, but every participant considers that their concerns have been taken seriously and can freely accept and implement the decision.[64]
6. Review of the Meeting
7. Closing Prayer of Gratitude

Within the process of discernment it is important to distinguish between what is variously referred to as decision-making and decision-taking, choice and decision, or a decision and its confirmation. The document from the Canadian Jesuits notes two kinds of confirmation: subjective confirmation, which is a sense of consolation about a decision reached; and objective confirmation, which comes from outside the group's experience. This may be from an external authority who has the final say on whether the grace of consensus and commitment is maintained during the implementation stage.[65] In the pair choice/decision, "choice" is the result of the discernment, and "decision" is the implementation of the choice.[66] A decision is only taken if there has been a confirmation of the choice. Sometimes one can also speak of a "provisionary decision" that precedes the "confirmation," which in turn precedes the "definite decision."[67] The pair decision-making/decision-taking are terms used in the *Instrumentum Laboris* for the 2023 assembly of the Synod on Synodality. Decision-making is the result of the discernment process and decision-taking is the action by the competent authority.[68] Obviously, the language is somewhat fluid, but whatever the terms, the result of communal discernment requires some kind of confirmation and may not be the definitive decision on the matter in terms of the action taken by the competent authority.

Apparent differences between the Futrell's model and the Canadian model include the systematic consideration of pros and cons in Futrell's model and a greater attention to movements of consolation and desolation beginning with the second round of sharing in the Canadian model. Attention to these movements appears to be limited to the sixth step of Futrell's model. His model provides for a more discursive general discussion absent from the other model. In part, this difference may be attributed to the fact that the Canadian model is a more general discernment process that can be further refined to make it a communal apostolic discernment, while the Futrell and Toner models seem to presuppose a more apostolic discernment committing the group to action.

Regardless of the model employed, in a successful communal discernment confirmed by the consolation of consensus, everyone has a sense of having been heard and the gifts and differences of each acknowledged. There is peace with the outcome, a sense that the process has been free and effective, and energy and empowerment to head into the future. There is a sense that the consensus has been the work of the Holy Spirit.[69]

Nevertheless, one must temper one's expectations of the results of the discernment, expecting modest results, for Orsy comments that what emerges is rarely "what is best in the group, but the standard that the majority of the members can somehow reach and grasp then and there."[70] Brilliant and prophetic outliers will probably not carry the day. Accepting less than the best may serve the unity of the group because the results do not get ahead of what people are capable of at a given time. Yet, because discernment is also not a leveling of a judgment down to the lowest common denominator acceptable to all, but the acceptance of a decision as what is best for the community at this time and place despite contrary opinions, discernment requires "the conversion of the community to the highest vision and to the most creative decision that emerges in the group."[71] Discernment may be a balance between what is best and what is possible, between no change or action and progress toward the next step in God's service and group conversion, between radical change and group unity and cohesiveness. Although discernment listens to the movements of the Spirit, it is also subject to human limitations. It is not necessarily perfect. Because it is historically conditioned, it too, is *in via*, on the way, representing a next step rather than the final step. Therefore, a successful discernment does not mean that the question discerned will never have to be reconsidered in the future. The outcome of any discernment process is fallible, subject to error, and limited by its cultural context, time in history, information available, and people involved. It may require future correction. While not negating a discernment at a given moment in time, any discernment is necessarily provisional and open-ended, open to further reexamination or adjustment as new data or circumstances arise.

CONCLUSION

Communal discernment was built into the process of the Synod on Synodality. However, both synodality and communal discernment are much more encompassing than the event of a synod in the life of the church. Pope Francis desires synodality and communal discernment to be built into the ethos of the church so that it becomes not an event, nor a set of convictions, but a lifestyle, a spirituality, and a "way of proceeding."[72] This means that discernment occurs not only during synods, but can be a way of proceeding for various groups such as parish councils, diocesan pastoral councils, governing boards, school faculties, religious communities, and diocesan and regional synods.[73] Discernment is not reserved to the spiritually elite, but is an activity for all those who serve in these venues.

A synodal church is schooled in the art of discernment in common and practices it at multiple levels of ecclesial life. While the Synod on Synodality placed discernment in common in the world's spotlight, its most effective use will likely be in local, smaller groups that can be more nimble in their habits of spiritual conversation and communal decision-making. The practice requires a cultural shift from a more parliamentarian approach to decision-making and the polarities inherent to the power dynamics of a political process to an approach of prayerful, respectful listening to the movements of the Spirit in one another and in the communal experience of the group. This shift is nothing less than a conversion and transformation of the church so that it may be a more effective evangelical witness to Christ's saving message of mercy.

NOTES

1. I use "communal discernment" and "discernment in common" as equivalent terms.
2. Bradford Hinze, *Practices of Dialogue in the Roman Catholic Church*, 256.
3. Diego Fares, SJ, "Aides pour grandir dan la capacité de discerner," in *Maturité Chrétienne et Discernement*, ed. Antonio Spadaro, SJ (Paris: Éditions Parole et Silence, 2019), 43–63, at 44.
4. David Lonsdale, SJ, *Dance to the Music of the Spirit* (London: Darton, Longman and Todd, 1992), 104.
5. The *Spiritual Exercises*, composed by St. Ignatius of Loyola (1522–1524), are comprised of Christian meditations, contemplations, and prayer divided into four thematic "weeks" of variable length. Designed to help exercitants to discern the will of God in their lives leading to a commitment to follow Jesus Christ, they provide rules for the discernment of spirits. *The Spiritual Exercises of Saint Ignatius,*

translation and commentary by George E. Gnass, SJ (Chicago: Loyola University Press, 1992), 313–36, 141–56. Hereafter *SpEx*.

6. Cited by Fares, "Aides pour grandir dan la capacité de discerner," 43. Francis makes this same point in *EG* 45.

7. Luke Timothy Johnson, *Scripture and Discernment: Decision Making in the Church* (Nashville: Abingdon Press, 1983), 110.

8. John Carroll Futrell, SJ, "Ignatian Discernment," *Studies in the Spirituality of Jesuits* 2 (1970): 47.

9. Ibid., 51.

10. Jules J. Toner, "A Method for Communal Discernment of God's Will," *Studies in the Spirituality of Jesuits* 3, no. 4 (1971): 124–25.

11. Fares, "Aides pour grandir dans la capacité de discerner," 45. English translation mine.

12. In his letter of December 25, 1971, Fr. General Pedro Arrupe, SJ, invited "all the members of the Society of Jesus to engage in an effort of communal discernment as a means of preparing for the order's next General Congregation." Gervais Dumeige, "Communal Discernment of Spirits and the Ignatian Method of Deliberation in a General Congregation," *The Way*, Supplement no. 20 (Autumn 1973): 55–71, at 71.

13. John Carroll Futrell, SJ, "Communal Discernment: Reflections on Experience," *Studies in the Spirituality of Jesuits* 4, no. 5 (November 1972): 159–92; Ladislas Orsy, SJ, "Toward a Theological Evaluation of Communal Discernment," *Studies in the Spirituality of Jesuits* 5, no. 5 (October 1973): 139–88; Toner, "A Method for Communal Discernment of God's Will," 124.

14. This meeting is possibly referenced in Galatians 2:1–2. Paul is informed of the decree in Acts 21:25, but qualified whether food offered to idols could be eaten out of consideration of another's conscience (1 Cor 10:27–29) and rejected other dietary restrictions (Gal 2:11–12; Col 2:21). Thus, there is some discrepancy from the account in Acts.

15. Rule of St. Benedict, chapter 3: On Calling the Brethren for Council, accessed July 23, 2024, http://archive.osb.org/rb/text/rbejms2.html#3.

16. See Section 3, "Decision-Making," in the *Quaker Handbook: The Handbook of Practice and Procedure* (New Zealand: Religious Society of Friends, 2022), https://quakers.nz/sites/default/files/documents/QHBook_Sept_2022_revised_edition.pdf.

17. Original Latin text in Monumenta Ignatiana, ser. 3, *Constitutiones 1* (Monumenta historica Societatis Iesu 63 (Rome: Gregoriana, 1934): 1–7. For English, see, among others, Jules J. Toner, "The Deliberation That Started the Jesuits: A Commentary on the *Deliberatio primorum partum*, Newly Translated with a Historical Introduction," *Studies in the Spirituality of Jesuits* 4 (1974): 179–212.

18. They had already vowed perpetual chastity and had made a vow of poverty before the legate of the pope when they were working among the Venetians.

19. Toner, "The Deliberation That Started the Jesuits," 205. Ladislas Orsy suggests that this may not have been a communal discernment in its full sense, insofar as Ignatius may have entered into it with a predetermined desire for permanent unity of the group of companions and consequently was not indifferent to the outcome of the process of deliberation. Ladislas Orsy, SJ, *Discernment: Theology and Practice, Communal and Personal* (Collegeville, MN: Liturgical Press, 2020), 17.

20. Francis, *EG* §§131–32.
21. International Theological Commission, "*Sensus Fidei* in the Life of the Church."
22. Thomas Aquinas, *Summa theologiae*, II–II, 34, 2.
23. Ibid., II–II, 45, 2.
24. Ibid.
25. Jacques Maritain, "On Knowledge through Connaturality," *Review of Metaphysics* 4 (1951): 473–74.
26. Ibid.
27. Jacques Maritain, *Man and the State* (Chicago: University of Chicago Press, 1951), 91–92.
28. Karl Rahner, *The Dynamic Element in the Church* (New York: Herder and Herder, 1964), 94.
29. Ibid., 102–3.
30. Ignatius, *SpEx* 2.
31. Orsy, "Toward a Theological Evaluation of Communal Discernment," 144.
32. Johnson, *Scripture and Discernment*, 132.
33. Futrell, "Communal Discernment," 167.
34. Orsy, "Toward a Theological Evaluation of Communal Discernment," 178.
35. Orsy, *Discernment*, 19.
36. Toner, "The Deliberation That Started the Jesuits," 187.
37. Orsy, *Discernment*, 24.
38. Jesuits of Canada, *Communal Apostolic Discernment: A Toolkit*, 9.
39. A good explanation of the examen and its steps based on George Aschenbrenner, *Consciousness Examen* (Wernersville, PA: Jesuit Center for Spiritual Growth, 2000) can be found at "Consciousness Examen by George Aschenbrenner, SJ" at https://prodigalcatholic.com/consciousness-examen-by-george-aschenbrenner-sj/.
40. Futrell, "Communal Discernment," 162.
41. Adolfo Nicolás, SJ, "Common Apostolic Discernment," *Review of Ignatian Spirituality* 40, no. 3 (2009): 9–20, at 18.
42. Francis, *EG*, §231–33.
43. Ignatius, *SpEx*, §170.
44. Futrell, "Communal Discernment," 171.
45. Summarized from Arturo Sosa, SJ, "Taking the Risk—Making Discernment Central," Discerning Leadership Programme, October 28, 2019, https://www.jesuits.global/2019/10/30/taking-the-risk-making-discernment-central/.
46. Jos Moons, SJ, "A Comprehensive Introduction to Synodality: Reconfiguring Ecclesiology and Ecclesial Practice," *Roczniki Theologiczne* 69, no. 2 (2022): 73–93, at 83.
47. Orsy, "Toward a Theological Evaluation of Communal Discernment," 173.
48. *SpEx*, §316.
49. Jesuits of Canada, *Communal Apostolic Discernment*, 67–68.
50. Futrell, "Communal Discernment," 164–65.
51. *SpEx* §317.
52. Jesuits of Canada, *Communal Apostolic Discernment*, 68.
53. *SpEx*, Rules for Second Week, 328–36.

54. *SpEx* §315.

55. John English, SJ, *Spiritual Intimacy and Community: An Ignatian View of the Small Faith Community* (London: Darton, Longman and Todd, 1992), 50.

56. Paul VI, Apostolic Exhortation, *Evangelii Nuntiandi*, December 8, 1975, 29, cited in Francis, *EG* 181.

57. Fares, "Aides pour grandir dans la capacité de discerner," 45.

58. "Ignatian Pedagogy: A Practical Approach," in *The Jesuit Ratio Studiorum of 1599*, ed. Vincent Duminuco (New York: Fordham University Press, 2000), appendix B, https://www.degruyter.com/document/doi/10.1515/9780823296866-014/html?lang=en.

59. Futrell, "Communal Discernment," 172–73. Futrell's model has many similarities to that of Toner, "A Method for Communal Discernment of God's Will," 121–52.

60. Jesuits of Canada, *Communal Apostolic Discernment*, 10–44.

61. "Ignatian Spiritual Exercises for the Corporate Person—Structured Resources for Group Development," compiled in James Borbely, *Focusing Group Energies: Common Ground for Leadership, Organization, Spirituality: Structures Resources for Group Development* (Scranton, PA: University of Scranton, 1992); also ESDAC, an abbreviation of Exercises Spirituels pour un Discernement Apostolique en Commun (Spiritual Exercises for Apostolic Discernment in Common), at https://jesuits.eu/join-the-mission/partners-in-mission/esdac. For discussion of how this might be applied in a secular context, see Michel Bacq, Laurent Falque, and Bernard Paulet, "Discerner en group," *Christus: Vivre l'Expérience Spirituelle Aujourd'hui, Le Discernement* 258 (May 2018): 180–90.

62. Futrell, "Communal Discernment," 172–73. See the entire article for further detail and commentary on the method.

63. See Jesuits of Canada, *Communal Apostolic Discernment*, which contains a much more detailed explanation of the components of spiritual conversations and communal apostolic discernment.

64. Ibid., 35.

65. Jesuits of Canada, *Communal Apostolic Discernment*, 41–42.

66. Bacq, Falque, and Paulet, "Discerner en group," 184.

67. Ibid., 185.

68. *IL*, First Session (October 2023), 52.

69. Ibid., 69.

70. Orsy, "Toward a Theological Evaluation of Communal Discernment," 165.

71. Ibid., 156.

72. Jos Moons, SJ, "Synodality and Discernment: The Affective Reconfiguration of the Church," *Studia Canonica* 56 (2022): 379–93, at 380. See additional bibliography in Dumeige, "Communal Discernment of Spirits and the Ignatian Method of Deliberation," 56.

73. See Eugene Duffy, "Processes for Communal Discernment: Diocesan Synods and Assemblies," *The Jurist* 71 (2011): 77–90.

Index

Abraham (biblical figure), 8, 51, 102
acolyte, 14–15, 38, 63–65
active listening, 4, 94–96, 108, 117
Acts of the Apostles, 9, 18, 27, 78, 119, 138n14
Ad Gentes (Decree on the Church's Missionary Activity), 30, 94
Afanasiev, Nicholas, 10–12, 24n14, 24n16, 24n19
Africa, 37, 54, 59
aggiornamento (updating traditions), 1
alienation, 76, 79, 89n21
Amazon Synod, 62
Amoris Laetitia (The Joy of Love) (Francis), 76
Anglicanorum Coetibus (Personal Ordinariates for Anglicans) (Benedict XVI), 37
Antiquum Ministerium (Francis), 64
Apostolicam Actuositatem (Decree on the Apostolate of the Laity), 15, 25n39, 49
Apostolica Sollicitudo (Paul VI), 57
apostolic constitution, 37, 57, 61, 108

Apostolic Council of Jerusalem (c. 48–50 AD), 1, 55, 119–20, 121
apostolic discernment, communal, 134–36
apostolic exhortation, 6n1, 15, 37, 62, 84, 107. *See also Evangelii Gaudium*
Apostolos Suos (John Paul II), 59, 61
Arrupe, General Pedro (Father), 138n12
Aschenbrenner, George, 139n39
Augustine (Saint), 9–10, 23n11

baptism, 7, 22; Eucharist and, 2–3; pilgrim church and, 75; with three interrelated processes, 74
baptismal ecclesiology, 2, 8–10, 12, 18, 20–22, 73
baptismal foundations: *Christifideles* and, 8–10, 15–17; conciliarity and synodality, 17–20, 23; ordering of community, 10–12; people of God in eucharistic assembly, 12–13; unity and differentiation within people of God, 14–15

baptismal spirituality, 73–75
Barnabas (biblical figure), 120
Bede (Saint), 80
Being as Communion (Zizioulas), 24n16
Benedictine monasticism, 119, 120–21
Benedictine order, 37
Benedict of Norcia (ca. 480–547) (Saint), 37
Benedict XVI (Joseph Ratzinger) (Pope), 37–38, 80, 107
Bergolio, Jorge, 38. *See also* Francis
Bonhoeffer, Dietrich, 90n53
Bread for the World, 83
Brouillette, André, 28, 32, 72

Canada, 61, 132, 134–35
canon law, 52, 56–57, 61–62
Caritas Internationalis, 83
Caritas in Veritate (Benedict XVI), 80
Catechism of the Catholic Church, 13, 37, 102
catechist, 14–15, 38, 54, 63–66
catechumenate, 74
Catholic Charities, 83
Catholic Relief Services, 83
Catholic Social Teaching, 134
charisms, 8, 11–12, 20, 22, 29, 85; discernment and, 5, 119, 122, 123–24, 127; Holy Spirit and, 14, 72; presidency as, 24n23. *See also communio*; *sensus fidei*; *sensus fidelium*
chastity, 126, 138n18
chrismation, 11, 24n14
Christian faithful. *See Christifideles*
Christianity, 37, 50–51, 52, 74–75, 119–20
Christifideles (Christian faithful), 7, 12, 23; within baptismal ecclesiology, 8–10; charisms of, 14; ecclesial context and secularity of, 15–17
Christifideles Laici (John Paul II), 15
1 Chronicles 16:22, 9
Chrysostom, John (Saint), 9, 19
church, 80; *Catechism of the Catholic Church*, 13, 37, 41, 102; *communio ecclesiarum*, 104–5; dialogue within, 94, 103–4; Eastern, 50, 52, 59; *Ecclesiam Suam*, 4, 93, 100, 110; Latin, 52, 70n43; Paul VI on secular mission of, 16; pyramid model of, 21, 55; "*Sensus Fidei* in the Life of the Church," 13, 124–25; *sentire cum ecclesia*, 19–20; synodal, 2, 4, 30, 58, 105; *For a Synodal Church*, 58; *Synodality in the Life and Mission of the Church*, 109; Synod on the Church in the Pan-Amazon Region, 106. *See also* diversity, within synodal church; pilgrim church
The Church of Mercy (Francis), 80
circuli minores (small working groups), 107, 108
City of God (Augustine), 23n11
clericalism, 14, 20–21, 87, 105
Code of Canon Law (*Codex Iuris Canonici*), 57
code of canon law, Eastern churches, 52
Codex Iuris Canonici. *See* Code of Canon Law
College of Cardinals, 61
Communal Apostolic Discernment (Jesuits of Canada), 134–35
communal discernment. *See* discernment in common
communio (communion), 122; discernment and, 127; *Episcopalis Communio*, 57, 108; eucharistic koinonia, 18, 20
communio ecclesiarum (communion of churches), 104–5
communio Episcoporum, 70n43
communio fidelium (communion of believers), 70n43, 104
communion: baptism and, 2; *Being as Communion*, 24n16; dialogue within ecclesiology of, 4, 104–6; diversity with structures to facilitate, 3–4, 55–62; ecclesial, 3–4, 22, 53, 61; ecclesiology, 3, 52–53, 55, 104; "organs of," 61–62; pilgrim church and journeying with others in, 41–43

communion of believers. *See communio fidelium*
communion of churches. *See communio ecclesiarum*
community: eucharistic, 11, 68n14; LGBTQ+, 76, 87, 130; ordering of baptismal, 10–12; priestly, 13
conciliarity, synodality and, 2, 17–20, 23
"Conclusions of the Special Synod of the Bishops of the Netherlands," 6n1
confession, sacramental, 89n21
Congar, Yves, 35, 39, 62, 105
Congregation for Divine Worship and the Sacraments. *See Liturgiam Authenticam*
connaturality, 5, 19, 125–27
consciousness examen, 129
consensus fidelium (consensus of the faithful), 13, 103, 127
consolation, apprehension of desolation and, 131–36
Constitution on the Liturgy. *See Sacrosanctum Concilium*
consultation process, Synod on Synodality, 58–59, 67
2 Corinthians: 1:21–22, 9; 13:4–7, 86
Costello, Jack, 33
The Cost of Discipleship (Bonhoeffer), 90n53
Council for the Economy, 38
Council of Jerusalem. *See* Apostolic Council of Jerusalem
Council of Nicaea (324 AD), 35
Council of Trent (1545–1563), 35, 84, 98, 100–101
culture: dialogue in pluralistic, 4, 98–100; dialogue with world, other faith traditions and, 4, 32, 94, 109–10
Cyprian (Bishop of Carthage), 18

data, discernment with judgment and, 130–31
death penalty, 41
De Bernadinis, Anke, 89n13

Decree on Ecumenism. *See Unitatis Redintegratio*
Decree on Religious Freedom (*Dignitatis Humanae*), 29, 97
Decree on Religious Life (*Perfectae Caritatis*), 119
Decree on the Apostolate of the Laity. *See Apostolicam Actuositatem*
Decree on the Church's Missionary Activity. *See Ad Gentes*
Decree on the Ministry and Life of Priests. *See Presbyterorum Ordinis*
Dei Verbum (Dogmatic Constitution on Divine Revelation), 29, 100–103, 125
De la Potterie, Ignace, 24n19
"The Deliberation That Started the Jesuits" (Toner), 138n19
de Lubac, Henri, 16
Derrida, Jacques, 51
Desiderio desideravi (Francis), 38
desolation, apprehension of consolation and, 131–36
destination, pilgrim church mission and, 29–32
Deus Caritas Est (Benedict XVI), 80
Deuteronomy, 101
dialogic speech, 94, 102–3
dialogue, 5, 43, 93, 111; within church, 94, 103–4; within ecclesiology of communion, 4, 104–6; with God, 4, 94, 100–103; intentional speaking and, 4, 96–97; nature of, 94–106; people of God and, 96, 98, 103–4; in pluralistic culture, 4, 98–100; spiritual conversations, 4, 117, 134–35, 137; synodality and, 106–9; with world, culture and other faith traditions, 4, 32, 94, 109–10
differentiation, 10, 13, 14–15, 22
Dignitatis Humanae. *See* Decree on Religious Freedom
discernment: of authentic reform and pilgrim church, 39–41; charisms and, 5, 119, 122, 123–24, 127; communal apostolic, 134–36; *communio* and, 127; communion ecclesiology and, 55; dialogue and,

5; Holy Spirit and, 118–29, 131, 136; Ignatius of Loyola and, 118, 122, 125, 127, 132–33, 137n5, 138n19; listening and, 95–96; on married priests, 62–63; mondialisation and, 67; with *sensus fidei* and *sensus fidelium*, 5, 122, 124–27; of spirits, 118–19, 123, 126, 137n5
discernment in common (communal discernment), 137n1; Apostolic Council of Jerusalem, 119–20; with apprehension of consolation and desolation, 131–36; Benedictine monasticism, 120–21; clarity about who makes final decision, 131; with data, 130–31; defined, 117, 118–19; elements, 119; examples, 119–22; identification of concrete object of, 129–30; interior freedom and, 128; with judgment, 118–19, 130–31; methods, 134–36; prayer and, 117, 122, 125, 128–29, 131, 134–35, 137n5; prerequisites for, 128–31; prior personal, 129; procedures, 133–34; Religious Society of Friends, 121–22; right people at table, 131; Society of Jesus and, 122; Synod on Synodality and, 137; theological foundations of, 122–31
Discipline of the Sacraments, 60
diversity, within synodal church: diversified ministries, 62–63; episcopal conferences, 59–61, 67; globalization and, 51–53, 60, 66; instituted ministries, 63–66; local church and, 50–51, 53–54, 58, 65–67; local structures, 61–62; mondialisation and, 51–54, 66–67; role of, 49–50; structures to facilitate communion within, 3–4, 55–62; synods, 56–59, 73
Dives in Misericordia (John Paul II), 80, 83
Divine Mercy Sunday, 80, 83
Dogmatic Constitution on Divine Revelation. *See Dei Verbum*

Dogmatic Constitution on the Church from the Second Vatican Council. *See Lumen Gentium*
Duffy, Stephen J., 81–82

Eastern churches, 50, 52, 59
Ecclesia in Africa (John Paul II), 37
Ecclesia in America (John Paul II), 37
Ecclesia in Asia (John Paul II), 37
Ecclesia in Europa (John Paul II), 37
Ecclesia in Oceania (John Paul II), 37
ecclesial communion, 3–4, 22, 53, 61
ecclesial humility, 4, 84–88
Ecclesiam Suam (On the Church) (Paul VI), 4, 93, 100, 110
ecumenical councils, 18, 36–37, 56
ecumenical movement, 2, 4
encyclicals: Benedict XVI with, 37; Francis, 80, 81; John Paul II, 37, 80, 83, 97; Paul VI, 4, 93, 100, 110; Pius XII, 103
English, John (Father), 133
Enlarge the Space of your Tent (Is. 54:2), 58, 59
Ephraim the Syrian (Saint), 112n21
episcopal conferences, 4, 54–56, 58, 63–65, 98, 106–8; with diversity within synodal church, 59–61, 67; Latin Church and, 70n43
Episcopalis Communio (Apostolic Constitution) (Francis), 57, 108
eschatology, 31
Une Espérance Nouvelle Pour le Liban (John Paul II), 37
Eucharist: baptism and, 2–3; *viaticum*, 32, 75, 76–77, 89n13
eucharistic assembly, 11, 12–13, 19
eucharistic communities, 11, 68n14
eucharistic koinonia. *See communio*
eucharistic spirituality, 4, 75–77
Eusebius (bishop of Caesarea), 9
Evangelii Gaudium (Francis): dialogue and, 96, 97, 110–11; discernment and, 118, 123–25, 130, 133; diversity and, 51, 60–61, 64; pilgrim church and, 30, 35, 37–40; spirituality and, 73, 76, 80, 84

Index

Evangelii nuntiandi (Paul VI), 37
evangelization, 35, 38, 64, 66, 84, 107, 110; baptism and, 22; new, 37, 67
evil, 39, 74, 80–81, 118–19, 133; forgiveness and, 83; sin and, 84, 130
examen, 129, 139n39

The Face of Mercy. *See Misericordiae Vultus*
faith. *See sensus fidei; sensus fidelium*
faith traditions, 4, 32, 94, 102, 109–10, 120, 122
Fares, Diego (Father), 119
Fastidius (Bishop), 10
Fessard, Gaston, 113n38
Fiducia Supplicans (On the Pastoral Meaning of Blessings) (Francis), 54, 130
First Ecumenical Council, 18
For a Synodal Church, 58
forgiveness, 79–83, 87, 100
Forte, Bruno, 8
Fox, George, 121
France, 56
Francis (Jorge Bergolio) (Pope), 21, 52, 56, 76, 113n38; apostolic constitution, 37, 57, 61, 108; in Canada, 61; on Christianity, 50, 51; on dialogue, 93–94, 105, 111; discernment and, 55, 129–30; encyclicals, 80, 81; episcopal conferences and, 61; on Eucharist, 89n13; *Fiducia Supplicans*, 54, 130; on Holy Spirit, 123; humility and, 85–86; on journey of church, 27; on listening, 95, 96, 99, 106; married priests and, 62–63; mercy and, 80–81, 83; "missionary option" and, 35; mondialisation and, 3; Motu Proprios, 64; on proselytism, 96–97; *sentire cum ecclesia* and, 19–20; on synodality, 1–2, 137; Synod on Synodality and, 57–58, 94, 119. *See also Evangelii Gaudium*
Francis of Assisi, 38
Fratelli Tutti (Francis), 80, 81

freedom, 28, 71–73, 75, 86, 96, 98–99, 132; discernment and, 128, 129; interior, 128; reconciliation, mercy and, 77–84; religious, 29, 36, 97; unfreedom, 79, 129
Futrell, John C. (Father), 118, 129, 132, 134–36

Galatians 2:1–2, 138n14
Gaudium et Spes (Pastoral Constitution of the Church in the Modern World), 15, 16, 30–31, 85, 94, 98
General Instruction of the Roman Missal, 13
Genesis 6:6, 81
globalization, 3, 6n6, 37, 51–53, 60, 66, 68nn6–7
God: dialogue with, 4, 94, 100–103; evil and, 81; mercy and, 8, 27, 30, 32, 34, 41, 43, 66, 71, 81–83, 86, 88, 123, 125, 127; will of, 5, 77–78, 118, 137n5. *See also* people of God
God's gracious presence to and concern for people. *See hānan*
Gospel Acclamation for Pentecost, 72
Grech, Mario (Cardinal), 57–58
Gregorian Reform, 35, 52
Guardini, Romano, 113n38

hānan (God's gracious presence to and concern for people), 81–82
Häring, Bernard, 79
hesed (mercy), 81–82
Holy Spirit, 7–8, 10, 22, 71, 86, 123; charisms and, 14, 72; *The Church of the Holy Spirit*, 24n14, 24n19; discernment and, 118–29, 131, 136; gift of, 19, 27, 73, 126; listening to, 94–95, 106, 109; mission of, 30; prayer and, 11, 55, 63, 85, 117, 134; receiving, 78–79; *sensus fidei* and, 19; *sensus fidelium* and, 103. *See also* charisms
Humani Generis (Pius XII), 103
humility, 4, 40, 71, 84–88, 95–96, 110, 120

Ignatian Spiritual Exercises for the Corporate Person. *See* ISECP
Ignatius of Loyola (Saint), 34; discernment and, 118, 122, 125, 127, 132–33, 137n5, 138n19; spirituality and, 33, 77
Imperatori-Lee, Natalia M., 50–51
indifference, 77–78, 93, 128
indigenous people, 61
instituted ministries, 2, 14–15, 38, 56, 63–67
Instrumentum Laboris, 42, 55–56, 58, 106–7; for Synod of Bishops, 50; for Synod on Synodality, 49, 53, 59, 61, 74, 108, 135
intentional speaking, 4, 96–97, 108, 117, 129
International Theological Commission, 13, 124–25
Irenaeus (Saint), 9
Isaiah, 8, 16, 78
ISECP (Ignatian Spiritual Exercises for the Corporate Person), 134
Israelites, 8, 28, 71, 73, 75, 77

Jacob of Serug, 112n21
James (biblical figure), 120
Jesuit General Congregation 36, 34
Jesuits, 33, 118–19, 122, 130, 132
Jesuits of Canada, 132, 134–35
Jews, 9, 87, 120
John (Saint), 100
John 4:19, 6:14, and 9:17, 9
John Paul II (Pope), 50, 107; apostolic exhortations, 6n1, 15, 37; on death penalty, 41; ecclesial communion and, 3; encyclicals, 37, 80, 83, 97; humility and, 86–87; mercy and, 80, 82–83; Motu Proprio, 59, 61; *Novo millennio ineunte*, 37; *Tertio millennio adveniente*, 37
Johnson, Luke Timothy, 118
John XXIII (Pope), 28, 84
journeying, 27–33, 41–43, 75, 76–77, 88, 89n13, 97
The Joy of Love. *See Amoris Laetitia*

judgment, 31, 56, 81, 85–88, 124–25, 136; discernment with, 118–19, 130–31; wisdom and, 126
justice, 9, 22, 28, 30–32, 81, 83–84, 88

Kasper, Walter (Cardinal), 7, 80, 82
1 Kings 19:16, 9
knowledge, connatural, 125–27
Komonchak, Joseph, 54

Lakeland, Paul, 85, 86
Latin church, 52, 70n43
Lazarus (biblical figure), 78
lector, 14–15, 38, 63–66
LGBTQ+ community, 76, 87, 130
Li, Victor, 51–52
limpia (purification) ritual, 61
Lineamenta (outline), 15, 58, 106
listening, 32, 58, 101, 109, 120–21; active, 4, 94–96, 108, 117; deep, 77, 86, 87–88, 119; mutual, 19, 99, 106, 132
Liturgiam Authenticam (Congregation for Divine Worship and the Sacraments), 60
Lonergan, Bernard, 39
Luciani, Rafael, 58
Luke: 4:24, 9; 5:33, 9–10
Lumen Gentium (Dogmatic Constitution on the Church from the Second Vatican Council), 3, 7–8, 14–17, 25n39, 50, 53, 103–4; discernment and, 123–24, 127; on people of God, 9, 19–20, 28; pilgrim church and, 29–33, 36, 40–42; on priestly community, 13; spirituality and, 71–72, 76–77, 85–86
Luther, Martin, 73–74
Lutherans, 4, 89n13

Mahler, Gustav, 27
Maritain, Jacques, 126
marriage, 36, 54, 62–63, 76, 106, 130
Mary (biblical figure), 28, 101, 102
maternal womb. *See rehem*
Matthew (Saint), 80

Merciful Like the Father. *See Misericordes Sicut Pater*
by mercifully choosing. *See Miserando atque eligendo*
mercy: *The Church of Mercy*, 80; *Dives in Misericordia*, 80, 83; Divine Mercy Sunday, 80, 83; freedom, reconciliation and, 77–84; God and, 8, 27, 30, 32, 34, 41, 43, 66, 71, 81–83, 86, 88, 123, 125, 137; *hesed*, 81–82; humility and, 4; *Miserando atque eligendo*, 80; *Misericordiae Vultus*, 83; *rahāmīm*, 81, 82
Mercy (Kasper), 80
Mexico City, 61
Micah 6:8, 84
Ministeria Quaedam (Paul VI), 63–64, 66
ministries: diversified, 62–63; instituted, 2, 14–15, 38, 56, 63–67; lay, 4, 14–16, 63–64
Miserando atque eligendo (by mercifully choosing), 80
Misericordes Sicut Pater (Merciful Like the Father), 83
Misericordiae Vultus (The Face of Mercy) (Francis), 83
mission: Paul VI on church and secular, 16; pilgrim church destination and, 29–32; *A Synodal Church in Mission*, 30; *Synodality in the Life and Mission of the Church*, 109
"missionary option," 35
mondialisation, 3, 6n6, 51–54, 66–67, 68nn6–7
money, 38, 81
Moons, Jos (Father), 131
Moses (biblical figure), 9
Motu Proprio, 37, 57, 59, 63–64

Nathaniel (biblical figure), 125
new evangelization, 37, 67
Nicolás, Adolfo (Father), 129
non-bishop members, Synod on Synodality, 57–58, 69n26
non-profit organizations, 83

Novo millennio ineunte (John Paul II), 37

O'Brien, John, 40
O'Gara, Margaret, 97
One Baptism (Wood), 2
On the Church. *See Ecclesiam Suam*
On the Pastoral Meaning of Blessings. *See Fiducia Supplicans*
On the Use of the Roman Liturgy Prior to the Reform of 1970. *See Traditionis Custodes*
Ordo Synodi Episcoporum Celebrandae, 57
"organs of communion," 61–62
Orsy, Ladislas, 128, 131–32, 136
Osheim, Amanda, 50–51
outline. *See Lineamenta*

Parable of the Good Samaritan, 81
Pastoral Constitution of the Church in the Modern World. *See Gaudium et Spes*
Paul (Saint), 55, 86, 118, 120, 123, 133, 138n14
Paul VI (Pope): apostolic exhortation, 37; on dialogue, 93–94; discernment and, 133; encyclicals, 4, 93, 100, 110; on listening, 94–95; Motu Proprios, 57, 63–64, 66; on secular mission of church, 16; Synod of Bishops and, 57, 94, 106
Pentecost, 72–73, 84
people of God: communion and, 3; defined, 8–9; dialogue and, 96, 98, 103–4; in eucharistic assembly, 12–13; Holy Spirit and, 73; *Lumen Gentium* on, 9, 19–20, 28; new, 7–9, 28–29; *sensus fidei* and, 58; unity and differentiation within, 14–15
Perfectae Caritatis (Decree on Religious Life), 119
Personal Ordinariates for Anglicans. *See Anglicanorum Coetibus*
Peter (biblical figure), 120
1 Peter: 2:9, 9; 2:9–10, 10, 18
Pharisees, 77

pilgrimage, 27, 29, 32–35, 71, 77–78, 87–88, 97
pilgrim church, 2–4, 7–8, 50–51; baptism and, 75; defined, 27–28; destination and mission, 29–32; discerning authentic reform, 39–41; journeying in communion with others, 41–43; journey of, 27, 32–33; transformation, reformation and purification, 33–39
Pius XII (Pope), 103
Plenary Councils of Baltimore, 106
pneumatological spirituality, 72–73, 121
Poland, 118
Pottmeyer, Hermann J., 104–5
poverty, 80, 138n18
Praedicate evangelium (Francis), 38, 61, 70n43
prayer, 9, 13, 18, 42, 62, 66, 72, 80; as dialogue, 94, 96; discernment in common and, 117, 122, 125, 128–29, 131, 134–35, 137n5; for forgiveness, 87; Holy Spirit and, 11, 55, 63, 85, 117, 134
Presbyterorum Ordinis (Decree on the Ministry and Life of Priests), 17
priesthood, 13, 21–22, 56; ordained, 2, 17, 63; royal, 9–12, 16–17, 23n11
proselytism, 96–97, 99
"provision for a journey." *See viaticum*
Psalm: 85:10, 84; 104, 72; 105:15, 9
purification, 3, 28, 31, 43, 72, 77, 117–18; dialogue and, 98; pilgrim church and, 33–39
purification ritual. *See limpia* ritual
pyramid model, of church, 21, 55

Quakers. *See* Religious Society of Friends
Querida Amazonia (Francis), 62

rahāmīm (mercy), 81, 82
Rahner, Karl, 109, 126
Ratzinger, Joseph, 103. *See also* Benedict XVI
Ravenna statement, 17–20

reconciliation, 4, 71, 74, 76, 88, 89n21, 104; freedom, mercy and, 77–84; sacrament of, 79
Redemptoris missio (John Paul II), 37
reform, 3, 33–34, 43, 61–62, 98, 106; Gregorian, 35, 52; pilgrim church and discerning authentic, 39–41; purification and, 31, 117–18; Vatican II, 36–38, 52
reformation, 33–39, 43, 72
rehem (maternal womb), 81, 82
Relatio post Disceptationem, 107
religious freedom, 29, 36, 97
Religious Society of Friends (Quakers), 121–22
ressourcement (return to sources of church tradition), 1
Rite of Institution, 65
Roman Curia, 61, 108
Romans 5:5, 72

sacramental confession, 89n21
sacramental theology, 75, 89n21
Sacrosanctum Concilium (Constitution on the Liturgy), 29, 60
St. Vincent de Paul Society, 83
same-sex marriage, 54
Sarah, Robert (Cardinal), 60
Scalfari, Eugenio, 97
Second Vatican Council. *See* Vatican II
sense of the faith. *See sensus fidei*
sense of the faithful. *See sensus fidelium*
sensus fidei (sense of the faith), 20, 113n33; dialogue and, 103, 109; discernment with *sensus fidelium* and, 5, 122, 124–27; Holy Spirit and, 19; people of God and, 58
"*Sensus Fidei* in the Life of the Church" (International Theological Commission), 13, 124–25
sensus fidelium (sense of the faithful), 5, 13, 103–4, 113n33, 122, 124–27
sentire cum ecclesia (to think and to feel with the church), 19–20
Septuagint, 81
shaman, 61

Index 149

sin, 31, 33, 39, 75–78, 87; evil and, 84, 130; forgiveness and, 80, 82; as unfreedom, 79

small working groups. *See circuli minores*

Society of Friends (Quakers). *See* Religious Society of Friends

Society of Jesus, 122, 129, 138n12

speaking: dialogic speech, 94, 102–3; intentional, 4, 96–97, 108, 117, 129

spirits, discernment of, 118–19, 123, 126, 137n5. *See also* Holy Spirit

spiritual conversations, 4, 117, 134–35, 137

spirituality, 2, 62, 137; baptismal, 73–75, 88n9; defined, 71; ecclesial humility and, 4, 84–88; eucharistic, 4, 75–77; with freedom, reconciliation and mercy, 77–84; Ignatius, 33, 77; pneumatological, 72–73, 121; as soul of synodal church, 4; "Towards a Spirituality for Synodality," 80

the *Spiritual Exercises* of Ignatius of Loyola (Ignatius of Loyola), 33, 34, 118, 127, 132, 137n5

Spiritus Domini (Francis), 64

Study Commission on the Diaconate of Women, 62

Summorum Pontificum (Benedict XVI), 37

A Synodal Church in Mission, 30

synodal church, 4, 30, 58; characteristics, 105; defined, 2. *See also* diversity, within synodal church

synodality: conciliarity and, 2, 17–20, 23; defined, 7, 30; dialogue and, 106–9; Francis on, 1–2, 137; "Towards a Spirituality for Synodality," 80. *See also* Synod on Synodality

Synodality in the Life and Mission of the Church, 109

Synod of Bishops, 4, 56, 108–9, 128; Benedict XVI and, 37; on "communion," 104; defined, 57; fiftieth anniversary celebration, 21, 106; *Instrumentum Laboris* for, 50; with inverted pyramid image, 21; *Lineamenta* for, 15; Paul VI and, 57, 94, 106; Synod on Synodality and, 67; Synod on Young People, 57, 106; voting members, 57–58

Synod on Synodality (2021–2024), 1, 5, 94, 106, 118, 119; consultation process, 58–59, 67; discernment in common and, 137; first session, 2, 29–30, 87; *Instrumentum Laboris* for second session, 49, 53, 59, 61, 74, 108, 135; listening sessions, 32, 58, 87; new model operative for, 58; non-bishop members, 57–58, 69n26; second session, 2, 49, 53, 59, 61, 74, 108, 135; Synod of Bishops and, 67; voting members, 57–58

Synod on the Church in the Pan-Amazon Region (2019), 106

Synod on Young People (2018), 106

synods: universal, 106; worldwide, 56–59, 73

Synods on Marriage and the Family (2014), 106

Synthesis Report, of Synod on Synodality, 29, 30

tax collector, 76, 80–81

Tertio millennio adveniente (John Paul II), 37

1 Thessalonians 5:19–20, 118

to think and to feel with the church. *See sentire cum ecclesia*

Thomas (Saint), 32, 125–26

Tomlin, Graham, 32

Toner, Jules J., 118, 136

tongues, 14, 27, 73, 78, 123

"Towards a Spirituality for Synodality," 80

Traditionis Custodes (On the Use of the Roman Liturgy Prior to the Reform of 1970) (Francis), 38

transformation, pilgrim church and, 33–39

unfreedom, 79, 129
Unitatis Redintegratio (Decree on Ecumenism), 29, 33, 99
United Nations, 6n6
United States Conference of Catholic Bishops, 106
unity, people of God with differentiation and, 14–15
updating traditions. *See aggiornamento*
Ut Unum sint (John Paul II), 37, 97

Vatican I, 84
Vatican II (Second Vatican Council) (1961–1965), 1, 4, 15, 34, 60, 62–63, 105, 108; aim of, 84; charisms and, 123; with church as pilgrim, 28; communion and, 104; dialogue and, 109; discernment and, 119; DV and, 29, 100–103, 125; with juxtapositions, 104; reform, 36–38, 52; on religious freedom, 97

viaticum ("provision for a journey"), 32, 75, 76–77, 89n13
Vincent of Lérins, 27
voting members: Synod of Bishops, 58; Synod on Synodality, 57–58

"We Are Witnesses of Christ Who Has Delivered Us," 6n1
will of God, 5, 77–78, 118, 137n5
wisdom, 19, 40, 96, 117, 123, 126, 129–30
Witherup, Ronald, 82–83
women, 9, 49, 57, 71, 74, 87, 127; diaconate open to, 54, 62; lay, 38, 64; shaman, 61
the world, dialogue with culture, other faith traditions and, 4, 32, 94, 109–10
World Youth Day, 34–35

Zechariah 7:9, 83–84
Zizioulas, John, 10–11, 24n16

About the Author

Susan K. Wood is professor of systematic theology at the Regis St. Michael's Faculty of Theology, Regis College, in the Toronto School of Theology at the University of Toronto. She received the John Courtney Murray Award from the Catholic Theological Society of America in 2021 in recognition of "outstanding and distinguished achievement in theology" and served as president of the CTSA, 2014–2015. She is co-moderator of the Peter and Paul Seminar and a member of the St. Irenaeus Working Group.

Very active in ecumenical work, Wood serves on the US Lutheran–Roman Catholic Dialogue (1994–present), the North American Roman Catholic–Orthodox Theological Consultation (2005–2023), the International Lutheran–Catholic Dialogue (2008–2019), and the conversation between the Baptist World Alliance and the Roman Catholic Church (2006–2010, 2017–2022). She serves on the editorial advisory boards of the journal *Ecclesiology* and the *Toronto Journal of Theology*. Most of her writing explores the connections between ecclesiology and sacramental theology.

Her publications include: *Spiritual Exegesis and the Church in the Theology of Henri de Lubac* (1998); *Sacramental Orders* (2000; 2008); *One Baptism: Ecumenical Dimensions of the Doctrine of Baptism* (2009); and with coauthor Timothy J. Wengert, *A Shared Spiritual Journey: Lutherans and Catholics Traveling toward Unity* (2016) in addition to numerous articles and book chapters.